Cram101 Textbook Outlines to accompany:

Essentials of Services Marketing: Concepts, Strategies, and Cases

Hoffman and Bateson, 2nd Edition

An Academic Internet Publishers (AIPI) publication (c) 2007.

Cram101 and Cram101.com are AIPI publications and services. All notes, highlights, reviews, and practice tests are prepared by AIPI for use in AIPI publications, all rights reserved.

You have a discounted membership at www.Cram101.com with this book.

Get all of the practice tests for the chapters of this textbook, and access in-depth reference material for writing essays and papers. Here is an example from a Cram101 Biology text:

When you need problem solving help with math, stats, and other disciplines, www.Cram101.com will walk through the formulas and solutions step by step.

STANDARD LOAN

Merthyr Tydfil Learning Resources Centre
Tel: (01685) 726005

Books are to be returned on or before the last date below

Merthyr Tydfil Learning Resources Centre CF48 1AR
University of Glamorgan

MERTHYR TYDFIL COLLEGE

17452

With Cram101.com online, you also have access to extensive reference material.

You will nail those essays and papers. Here is an example from a Cram101 Biology text:

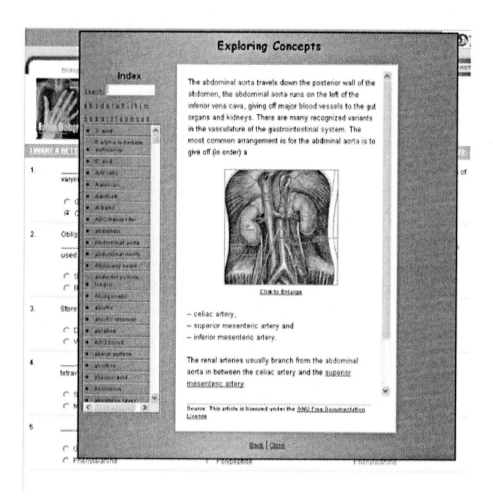

Visit **www.Cram101.com**, click Sign Up at the top of the screen, and enter DK73DW in the promo code box on the registration screen. Access to www.Cram101.com is normally $9.95, but because you have purchased this book, your access fee is only $4.95. Sign up and stop highlighting textbooks forever.

Learning System

Cram101 Textbook Outlines is a learning system. The notes in this book are the highlights of your textbook, you will never have to highlight a book again.

How to use this book. Take this book to class, it is your notebook for the lecture. The notes and highlights on the left hand side of the pages follow the outline and order of the textbook. All you have to do is follow along while your intructor presents the lecture. Circle the items emphasized in class and add other important information on the right side. With Cram101 Textbook Outlines you'll spend less time writing and more time listening. Learning becomes more efficient.

Cram101.com Online

Increase your studying efficiency by using Cram101.com's practice tests and online reference material. It is the perfect complement to Cram101 Textbook Outlines. Use self-teaching matching tests or simulate in-class testing with comprehensive multiple choice tests, or simply use Cram's true and false tests for quick review. Cram101.com even allows you to enter your in-class notes for an integrated studying format combining the textbook notes with your class notes.

Visit **www.Cram101.com**, click Sign Up at the top of the screen, and enter **DK73DW554** in the promo code box on the registration screen. Access to www.Cram101.com is normally $9.95, but because you have purchased this book, your access fee is only $4.95. Sign up and stop highlighting textbooks forever.

Copyright © 2007 by Academic Internet Publishers, Inc. All rights reserved. "Cram101"® and "Never Highlight a Book Again!"® are registered trademarks of Academic Internet Publishers, Inc. The Cram101 Textbook Outline series is printed in the United States. ISBN: 1-4288-0657-1

Essentials of Services Marketing: Concepts, Strategies, and Cases
Hoffman and Bateson, 2nd

CONTENTS

Marketing	The American Marketing Association suggests that Marketing is "the process of planning and executing the pricing, promotion, and distribution of goods, ideas, and services to create exchanges that satisfy individual and organizational goals."
Economy	The income, expenditures, and resources that affect the cost of running a business and household are called an economy.
Insurance	A means for persons and businesses to protect themselves against the risk of loss is insurance.
Revenue	Revenue refers to the total amount of money a business earns in a given period by selling goods and services. The value of what is received for goods sold, services rendered.
Tangible	Having a physical existence is referred to as the tangible. Personal property other than real estate, such as cars, boats, stocks, or other assets.
Competition	In business, competition occurs when rival organizations with similar products and services attempt to gain customers.
Industry	Industry refers to a group of firms offering products that are close substitutes for each other.
Lease	A contract for the possession and use of land or other property, including goods, on one side, and a recompense of rent or other income on the other is the lease.
Acceleration	Acceleration refers to the shortening of the time for the performance of a contract or the payment of a note by the operation of some provision in the contract or note itself.
Customer service	The ability of logistics management to satisfy users in terms of time, dependability, communication, and convenience is called the customer service.
Options	Options give the owner the right but not the obligation to buy or sell an underlying security at a set price for a given time period.
Product	Any physical good, service, or idea that satisfies a want or need is called product. Product in project management is a physical entity created as a result of project work.
Remainder	A remainder in property law is a future interest created in a transferee that is capable of becoming possessory upon the natural termination of a prior estate created by the same instrument.
Competitive Strategy	An outline of how a business intends to compete with other firms in the same industry is called competitive strategy.
Production	The creation of finished goods and services using the factors of production: land, labor, capital, entrepreneurship, and knowledge.
Premium	Premium refers to the fee charged by an insurance company for an insurance policy. The rate of losses must be relatively predictable: In order to set the premium (prices) insurers must be able to estimate them accurately.
Policy	Similar to a script in that a policy can be a less than completely rational decision-making method. Involves the use of a pre-existing set of decision steps for any problem that presents itself.
Competitor	Other organizations in the same industry or type of business that provide a good or service to the same set of customers is referred to as a competitor.
Property	Property refers to something that is capable of being owned. A right or interest associated with something that gives the owner the ability to exercise dominion over it.
Intangibility	A unique element of services-services cannot be held, touched, or seen before the purchase decision which is referred to as intangibility.
Purchasing	Purchasing refers to the function in a firm that searches for quality material resources, finds the best suppliers, and negotiates the best price for goods and services.

Go to **Cram101.com** for the Practice Tests for this Chapter.

Go to **Cram101.com** for the Practice Tests for this Chapter.
And, **NEVER** highlight a book again!

Cost of goods sold	A measure of the cost of merchandise sold or cost of raw materials and supplies used for producing items for resale is called cost of goods sold.
Stock	In financial terminology, stock is the capital raized by a corporation, through the issuance and sale of shares. A shareholder is any person or organization which owns one or more shares of a corporation's stock. The aggregate value of a corporation's issued shares is its market capitalization.
Markup	Markup is a term used in marketing to indicate how much the price of a product is above the cost of producing and distributing the product.
Experience Economy	Economy in which companies compete for customers by offering enjoyable, memorable experiences rather than traditional service transactions is referred to as experience economy.
Complexity	The technical sophistication of the product and hence the amount of understanding required to use it is referred to as complexity. It is the opposite of simplicity.
Management	Management characterizes the process of leading and directing all or part of an organization, often a business, through the deployment and manipulation of resources. Early twentieth-century management writer Mary Parker Follett defined management as "the art of getting things done through people."
Possession	Possession refers to respecting real property, exclusive dominion and control such as owners of like property usually exercise over it. Manual control of personal property either as owner or as one having a qualified right in it.
Positioning	The art and science of fitting the product or service to one or more segments of the market in such a way as to set it meaningfully apart from competition is called positioning.
Manager	A person who is formally responsible for supporting the work efforts of other people is a manager.
Personnel	A collective term for all of the employees of an organization. Personnel is also commonly used to refer to the personnel management function or the organizational unit responsible for administering personnel programs.
Contact personnel	The people at the 'front lines' who interact with the public in a service setting are contact personnel.
Customer contact	Customer contact refers to a characteristic of services that notes that customers tend to be more involved in the production of services than they are in manufactured goods.
Standing	Standing refers to the legal requirement that anyone seeking to challenge a particular action in court must demonstrate that such action substantially affects his legitimate interests before he will be entitled to bring suit.
Hearing	A hearing is a proceeding before a court or other decision-making body or officer. A hearing is generally distinguished from a trial in that it is usually shorter and often less formal.
Discount	A discount is the reduction of the base price of a product.
Participation	Participation refers to the process of giving employees a voice in making decisions about their own work.
Contribution	In business organization law, the cash or property contributed to a business by its owners is referred to as contribution.
Deregulation	Deregulation refers to government withdrawal of certain laws and regulations that seem to hinder competition.
Gross domestic product	The total value of goods and services produced in a country in a given year is a gross domestic product. It is one of several measures of the size of its economy.
Interest	Interest refers to the payment the issuer of the bond makes to the bondholders for use of the borrowed money. It is the return to capital achieved over time or as the result of an event.

Go to **Cram101.com** for the Practice Tests for this Chapter.

Go to **Cram101.com** for the Practice Tests for this Chapter.
And, **NEVER** highlight a book again!

E-commerce	The sale of goods and services by computer over the Internet is referred to as the e-commerce.
Brand	A name, symbol, or design that identifies the goods or services of one seller or group of sellers and distinguishes them from the goods and services of competitors is a brand.
Budget	A financial plan that sets forth management's expectations for revenues and, based on those expectations, allocates the use of specific resources throughout the firm is called budget.
Agency	Agency refers to a legal relationship in which an agent acts under the direction of a principal for the principal's benefit. Also used to refer to government regulatory bodies of all kinds.
Accounting	The recording, classifying, summarizing, and interpreting of financial events and transactions to provide management and other interested parties the information they need to make good decisions is called accounting.
Value added	Dimension of the retail-positioning matrix that refers to elements such as location, product reliability, or prestige is value added.
Human capital	The economic value of the knowledge, experience, skills, and capabilities of employees is called human capital.
Capital	Contributions of money and other property to a business made by the owners of the business are capital.
Gross national product	Gross national product refers to the market value of all the final goods and services produced by a national economy.
Exporter	A firm that sells its product in another country is an exporter.
Balance of payments	The balance of payments is a measure of the payments that flow into and out from a particular country from and to other countries. It is determined by a country's exports and imports of goods, services, and financial capital, as well as financial transfers.
Customer retention	Customer retention refers to the percentage of customers who return to a service provider or continue to purchase a manufactured product.
Promotion	Promotion refers to all the techniques sellers use to motivate people to buy products or services. An attempt by marketers to inform people about products and to persuade them to participate in an exchange.
Advertising	Advertising refers to paid, nonpersonal communication through various media by organizations and individuals who are in some way identified in the advertising message.
Productivity	Productivity refers to the total output of goods and services in a given period of time divided by work hours.
Asset	In business and accounting an asset is anything owned which can produce future economic benefit, whether in possession or by right to take possession, by a person or a group acting together, e.g. a company, the measurement of which can be expressed in monetary terms. Asset is listed on the balance sheet. It has a normal balance of debit.
Content	Content refers to all digital information included on a website, including the presentation form-text, video, audio, and graphics.
Compensation	A payment that is given or recieved as reparation for a service or loss is referred to as compensation.
Generally accepted accounting principles	Standards for the preparation and presentation of financial statements are called generally accepted accounting principles.
Human resources	Human resources refers to the individuals within the firm, and to the portion of the firm's organization that deals with hiring, firing, training, and other personnel issues.

Go to Cram101.com for the Practice Tests for this Chapter.

Go to **Cram101.com** for the Practice Tests for this Chapter.
And, **NEVER** highlight a book again!

International trade	The export of goods and services from a country and the import of goods and services into a country is referred to as the international trade.
Retailing	All activities involved in selling, renting, and providing goods and services to ultimate consumers for personal, family, or household use is referred to as retailing.

Go to **Cram101.com** for the Practice Tests for this Chapter.
And, **NEVER** highlight a book again!

Intangibility	A unique element of services-services cannot be held, touched, or seen before the purchase decision which is referred to as intangibility.
Marketing	The American Marketing Association suggests that Marketing is "the process of planning and executing the pricing, promotion, and distribution of goods, ideas, and services to create exchanges that satisfy individual and organizational goals."
Inseparability	Inseparability is a characteristic of services, which describes how service products tend to be produced at the same time as they are consumed.
Target market	One or more specific groups of potential consumers toward which an organization directs its marketing program are a target market.
Production	The creation of finished goods and services using the factors of production: land, labor, capital, entrepreneurship, and knowledge.
Tangible	Having a physical existence is referred to as the tangible. Personal property other than real estate, such as cars, boats, stocks, or other assets.
Purchasing	Purchasing refers to the function in a firm that searches for quality material resources, finds the best suppliers, and negotiates the best price for goods and services.
Possession	Possession refers to respecting real property, exclusive dominion and control such as owners of like property usually exercise over it. Manual control of personal property either as owner or as one having a qualified right in it.
Patent	A patent is a set of exclusive rights granted by a state to a person for a fixed period of time in exchange for the regulated, public disclosure of certain details of a device, method, process or composition of matter which is new, inventive, and useful or industrially applicable.
Inventory	Inventory refers to physical material purchased from suppliers, which may or may not be reworked for sale to customers. A unique element of services-the need for and cost of having a service provider available.
Bottom line	Bottom line refers to the last line in a profit and loss statement; it refers to net profit.
Property	Property refers to something that is capable of being owned. A right or interest associated with something that gives the owner the ability to exercise dominion over it.
Competitor	Other organizations in the same industry or type of business that provide a good or service to the same set of customers is referred to as a competitor.
Promotion	Promotion refers to all the techniques sellers use to motivate people to buy products or services. An attempt by marketers to inform people about products and to persuade them to participate in an exchange.
Product	Any physical good, service, or idea that satisfies a want or need is called product. Product in project management is a physical entity created as a result of project work.
Insurance	A means for persons and businesses to protect themselves against the risk of loss is insurance.
Industry	Industry refers to a group of firms offering products that are close substitutes for each other.
Cost-plus pricing	The practice of summing the total unit cost of providing a product or service and adding a specific amount to the cost to arrive at a price is referred to as cost-plus pricing.
Pricing	Pricing is the manual or automatic process of applying prices to purchase and sales orders, based on factors such as: a fixed amount, quantity break, promotion or sales campaign, specific vendor quote, price prevailing on entry, shipment or invoice date, combination of

Go to **Cram101.com** for the Practice Tests for this Chapter.

Go to **Cram101.com** for the Practice Tests for this Chapter.
And, **NEVER** highlight a book again!

	multiple orders or lines, and many others.
Markup	Markup is a term used in marketing to indicate how much the price of a product is above the cost of producing and distributing the product.
Cost of goods sold	A measure of the cost of merchandise sold or cost of raw materials and supplies used for producing items for resale is called cost of goods sold.
Personnel	A collective term for all of the employees of an organization. Personnel is also commonly used to refer to the personnel management function or the organizational unit responsible for administering personnel programs.
Policy	Similar to a script in that a policy can be a less than completely rational decision-making method. Involves the use of a pre-existing set of decision steps for any problem that presents itself.
Advertising	Advertising refers to paid, nonpersonal communication through various media by organizations and individuals who are in some way identified in the advertising message.
Stock	In financial terminology, stock is the capital raized by a corporation, through the issuance and sale of shares. A shareholder is any person or organization which owns one or more shares of a corporation's stock. The aggregate value of a corporation's issued shares is its market capitalization.
Incentive	A reward offered by a marketer to a prospective customer in return for furnishing information or making a purchase is referred to as an incentive.
Mass media	Mass media refers to non-personal channels of communication that allow a message to be sent to many individuals at one time.
Perceived risk	The anxieties felt because the consumer cannot anticipate the outcomes of a purchase but believes that there may be negative consequences is called a perceived risk.
Agent	One who acts under the direction of a principal for the principal's benefit in a legal relationship known as agency is called agent.
Brand awareness	How quickly or easily a given brand name comes to mind when a product category is mentioned is brand awareness.
Brand	A name, symbol, or design that identifies the goods or services of one seller or group of sellers and distinguishes them from the goods and services of competitors is a brand.
Evaluation	The consumer's appraisal of the product or brand on important attributes is called evaluation.
Communication	Communication refers to the social process in which two or more parties exchange information and share meaning.
Contact personnel	The people at the 'front lines' who interact with the public in a service setting are contact personnel.
Internal customer	An individuals or unit within the firm that receives services from other entities within the organization is an internal customer.
Participation	Participation refers to the process of giving employees a voice in making decisions about their own work.
Customer contact	Customer contact refers to a characteristic of services that notes that customers tend to be more involved in the production of services than they are in manufactured goods.
Efficiency	Efficiency refers to the use of minimal resources, such as raw materials, money, and people- to produce a desired volume of output.

Go to **Cram101.com** for the Practice Tests for this Chapter.

Go to **Cram101.com** for the Practice Tests for this Chapter.
And, **NEVER** highlight a book again!

Customer service	The ability of logistics management to satisfy users in terms of time, dependability, communication, and convenience is called the customer service.
Manager	A person who is formally responsible for supporting the work efforts of other people is a manager.
Management	Management characterizes the process of leading and directing all or part of an organization, often a business, through the deployment and manipulation of resources. Early twentieth-century management writer Mary Parker Follett defined management as "the art of getting things done through people."
Market segments	Market segments refer to the groups that result from the process of market segmentation; these groups ideally have common needs and will respond similarly to a marketing action.
Contract	A contract is a "promise" or an "agreement" that is enforced or recognized by the law. In the civil law, contracts are considered to be part of the general law of obligations. This article describes the law relating to contracts in common law jurisdictions.
Voice of the customer	A term that refers to the wants, opinions, perceptions, and desires of the customer is a voice of the customer.
Bond	A long-term debt security that is secured by collateral is called a bond.
Mass production	The process of making a large number of a limited variety of products at very low cost is referred to as mass production.
Exhibit	Exhibit refers to a copy of a written instrument on which a pleading is founded, annexed to the pleading and by reference made a part of it. Any paper or thing offered in evidence and marked for identification.
Public relations	Public relations refers to the management function that evaluates public attitudes, changes policies and procedures in response to the public's requests, and executes a program of action and information to earn public understanding and acceptance.
Trust	Trust refers to a legal relationship in which a person who has legal title to property has the duty to hold it for the use or benefit of another person. The term is also used in a general sense to mean confidence reposed in one person by another.
Empathy	Empathy refers to dimension of service quality-caring individualized attention provided to customers.
Core	A core is the set of feasible allocations in an economy that cannot be improved upon by subset of the set of the economy's consumers (a coalition).
Accounting	The recording, classifying, summarizing, and interpreting of financial events and transactions to provide management and other interested parties the information they need to make good decisions is called accounting.
Staffing	Staffing refers to a management function that includes hiring, motivating, and retaining the best people available to accomplish the company's objectives.
Client	The organizations with the products, services, or causes to be marketed and for which advertising agencies and other marketing promotional firms provide services is referred to as a client.
Franchise	A business established or operated under an authorization to sell or distribute a company's goods or services in a particular area is a franchise.
Quality control	The measurement of products and services against set standards is referred to as quality control.
Variance	In budgeting a variance is a difference between budgeted, planned or standard amount and the

Go to **Cram101.com** for the Practice Tests for this Chapter.

Go to **Cram101.com** for the Practice Tests for this Chapter.
And, **NEVER** highlight a book again!

actual amount incurred/sold.

Appeal	Appeal refers to the act of asking an appellate court to overturn a decision after the trial court's final judgment has been entered.
Options	Options give the owner the right but not the obligation to buy or sell an underlying security at a set price for a given time period.
Channel	Channel, in communications (sometimes called communications channel), refers to the medium used to convey information from a sender (or transmitter) to a receiver.
Distribution	Distribution is one of the four aspects of marketing. A distribution business is the middleman between the manufacturer and retailer or (usually)in commercial or industrial the business customer.
Consumer behavior	Consumer behavior refers to the actions a person takes in purchasing and using products and services, including the mental and social processes that precede and follow these actions.
Consumer	A consumer is a individual or household that consume goods and services generated within the economy. Since this includes just about everyone, the term is a political term as much as an economic term when it is used in everyday speech.
Transfer price	The price at which goods and services are transferred between subsidiary companies of a corporation is referred to as the transfer price.
Level of service	The degree of service provided to the customer by self, limited, and full-service retailers is referred to as the level of service.
Publicity	Publicity refers to any information about an individual, product, or organization that's distributed to the public through the media and that's not paid for or controlled by the seller.
Bankruptcy	The state of a person who is unable to pay his or her debts without respect to time is called bankruptcy.
Standing	Standing refers to the legal requirement that anyone seeking to challenge a particular action in court must demonstrate that such action substantially affects his legitimate interests before he will be entitled to bring suit.
Revenue	Revenue refers to the total amount of money a business earns in a given period by selling goods and services. The value of what is received for goods sold, services rendered.
Tangibles	Dimension of service quality-appearance of physical facilities, equipment, personnel, and communication materials are called tangibles.
Preparation	Preparation refers to usually the first stage in the creative process. It includes education and formal training.
Organizational commitment	A person's identification with and attachment to an organization is called organizational commitment.
Billboard	The most common form of outdoor advertising is called a billboard.
Preference	The act of a debtor in paying or securing one or more of his creditors in a manner more favorable to them than to other creditors or to the exclusion of such other creditors is a preference. In the absence of statute, a preference is perfectly good, but to be legal it must be bona fide, and not a mere subterfuge of the debtor to secure a future benefit to himself or to prevent the application of his property to his debts.
Retailing	All activities involved in selling, renting, and providing goods and services to ultimate consumers for personal, family, or household use is referred to as retailing.

Go to **Cram101.com** for the Practice Tests for this Chapter.
And, **NEVER** highlight a book again!

Marketing	The American Marketing Association suggests that Marketing is "the process of planning and executing the pricing, promotion, and distribution of goods, ideas, and services to create exchanges that satisfy individual and organizational goals."
Intangibility	A unique element of services-services cannot be held, touched, or seen before the purchase decision which is referred to as intangibility.
Inseparability	Inseparability is a characteristic of services, which describes how service products tend to be produced at the same time as they are consumed.
Industry	Industry refers to a group of firms offering products that are close substitutes for each other.
Insurance	A means for persons and businesses to protect themselves against the risk of loss is insurance.
Competition	In business, competition occurs when rival organizations with similar products and services attempt to gain customers.
Competitor	Other organizations in the same industry or type of business that provide a good or service to the same set of customers is referred to as a competitor.
Best practice	In business management, a best practice is a generally accepted "best way of doing a thing". A best practice is formulated after the study of specific business or organizational case studies to determine the most broadly effective and efficient means of organizing a system or performing a function.
Warehouse	Warehouse refers to a location, often decentralized, that a firm uses to store, consolidate, age, or mix stock; house product-recall programs; or ease tax burdens.
Production	The creation of finished goods and services using the factors of production: land, labor, capital, entrepreneurship, and knowledge.
Benchmarking	Discovering how others do something better than your own firm so you can imitate or leapfrog competition is called benchmarking.
Asset	In business and accounting an asset is anything owned which can produce future economic benefit, whether in possession or by right to take possession, by a person or a group acting together, e.g. a company, the measurement of which can be expressed in monetary terms. Asset is listed on the balance sheet. It has a normal balance of debit.
Product	Any physical good, service, or idea that satisfies a want or need is called product. Product in project management is a physical entity created as a result of project work.
Shopping good	An item for which the consumer compares several alternatives on criteria such as price, quality, or style is called a shopping good.
Category killers	Category killers refer to specialty discount outlets that focus on one type of product, such as electronics or business supplies, at very competitive prices. They often dominate the market.
Category killer	Category killer is a term used in marketing and strategic management to describe a product, service, brand, or company that has such a distinct sustainable competitive advantage that competing firms find it almost impossible to operate profitably in that industry. The existence of a category killer will eliminate almost all market entity, whether real or virtual.
Promotion	Promotion refers to all the techniques sellers use to motivate people to buy products or services. An attempt by marketers to inform people about products and to persuade them to participate in an exchange.

Go to **Cram101.com** for the Practice Tests for this Chapter.

Go to **Cram101.com** for the Practice Tests for this Chapter.
And, **NEVER** highlight a book again!

Evaluation	The consumer's appraisal of the product or brand on important attributes is called evaluation.
Purchasing	Purchasing refers to the function in a firm that searches for quality material resources, finds the best suppliers, and negotiates the best price for goods and services.
Agent	One who acts under the direction of a principal for the principal's benefit in a legal relationship known as agency is called agent.
Personnel	A collective term for all of the employees of an organization. Personnel is also commonly used to refer to the personnel management function or the organizational unit responsible for administering personnel programs.
Agency	Agency refers to a legal relationship in which an agent acts under the direction of a principal for the principal's benefit. Also used to refer to government regulatory bodies of all kinds.
Preparation	Preparation refers to usually the first stage in the creative process. It includes education and formal training.
Downsizing	The process of eliminating managerial and non-managerial positions are called downsizing.
Corporation	A form of business organization that is owned by owners, called shareholders, who have no inherent right to manage the business, and is managed by a board of directors that is elected by the shareholders is called a corporation.
Client	The organizations with the products, services, or causes to be marketed and for which advertising agencies and other marketing promotional firms provide services is referred to as a client.
Advertising	Advertising refers to paid, nonpersonal communication through various media by organizations and individuals who are in some way identified in the advertising message.
Economies of scale	A decline in costs with accumulated sales or production is an economies of scale. In advertising, economies of scale often occur in media purchases as the relative costs of advertising time and/or space may decline as the size of the media budget increases.
Incentive	A reward offered by a marketer to a prospective customer in return for furnishing information or making a purchase is referred to as an incentive.
Mass media	Mass media refers to non-personal channels of communication that allow a message to be sent to many individuals at one time.
Accounting	The recording, classifying, summarizing, and interpreting of financial events and transactions to provide management and other interested parties the information they need to make good decisions is called accounting.
Litigation	The process of bringing, maintaining, and defending a lawsuit is litigation.
Intellectual property	Products of the mind, ideas. Intellectual property can be protected by patents, copyrights, and trademarks.
Property	Property refers to something that is capable of being owned. A right or interest associated with something that gives the owner the ability to exercise dominion over it.
Standard of living	The amount of goods and services people can buy with the money they have is called standard of living.
Market segments	Market segments refer to the groups that result from the process of market segmentation; these groups ideally have common needs and will respond similarly to a marketing action.
Economy	The income, expenditures, and resources that affect the cost of running a business and

Go to **Cram101.com** for the Practice Tests for this Chapter.
And, **NEVER** highlight a book again!

household are called an economy.

Recession	Two or more consecutive quarters of decline in the Gross Domestic Product is referred to as a recession.
Appeal	Appeal refers to the act of asking an appellate court to overturn a decision after the trial court's final judgment has been entered.
Interest	Interest refers to the payment the issuer of the bond makes to the bondholders for use of the borrowed money. It is the return to capital achieved over time or as the result of an event.
Trust	Trust refers to a legal relationship in which a person who has legal title to property has the duty to hold it for the use or benefit of another person. The term is also used in a general sense to mean confidence reposed in one person by another.
Revenue	Revenue refers to the total amount of money a business earns in a given period by selling goods and services. The value of what is received for goods sold, services rendered.
Users	Users refer to people in the organization who actually use the product or service purchased by the buying center.
Information technology	Information technology refers to technology that helps companies change business by allowing them to use new methods.
Stock	In financial terminology, stock is the capital raized by a corporation, through the issuance and sale of shares. A shareholder is any person or organization which owns one or more shares of a corporation's stock. The aggregate value of a corporation's issued shares is its market capitalization.
Context	The effect of the background under which a message often takes on more and richer meaning is a context. Context is especially important in cross-cultural interactions because some cultures are said to be high context or low context.
Enterprise resource planning	Computer-based production and operations system that links multiple firms into one integrated production unit is enterprise resource planning.
Market space	Market space is an internet-Web-enabled digital environment characterized by 'face-to-screen' exchange relationships and electronic images and offerings.
Content	Content refers to all digital information included on a website, including the presentation form-text, video, audio, and graphics.
Distribution	Distribution is one of the four aspects of marketing. A distribution business is the middleman between the manufacturer and retailer or (usually)in commercial or industrial the business customer.
Lease	A contract for the possession and use of land or other property, including goods, on one side, and a recompense of rent or other income on the other is the lease.
Commerce	Commerce is the exchange of something of value between two entities. It is the central mechanism from which capitalism is derived.
Procurement	Procurement is the acquisition of goods or services at the best possible total cost of ownership, in the right quantity, at the right time, in the right place for the direct benefit or use of the governments, corporations, or individuals generally via, but not limited to a contract.
Supply-chain management	Supply-chain management refers to the process of managing the movement of raw materials, parts, work in progress, finished goods, and related information through all the organizations involved in the supply chain; managing the return of such goods, if necessary.

Go to **Cram101.com** for the Practice Tests for this Chapter.
And, **NEVER** highlight a book again!

Management	Management characterizes the process of leading and directing all or part of an organization, often a business, through the deployment and manipulation of resources. Early twentieth-century management writer Mary Parker Follett defined management as "the art of getting things done through people."
E-business	E-business refers to work an organization does using electronic linkages; any business that takes place by digital processes over a computer network rather than in a physical space.
E-commerce	The sale of goods and services by computer over the Internet is referred to as the e-commerce.
Product mix	The combination of product lines offered by a manufacturer is referred to as product mix.
Manager	A person who is formally responsible for supporting the work efforts of other people is a manager.
Browser	A program that allows a user to connect to the World Wide Web by simply typing in a URL is a browser.
Buyer	A buyer refers to a role in the buying center with formal authority and responsibility to select the supplier and negotiate the terms of the contract.
Brand	A name, symbol, or design that identifies the goods or services of one seller or group of sellers and distinguishes them from the goods and services of competitors is a brand.
Forming	The first stage of team development, where the team is formed and the objectives for the team are set is referred to as forming.
Bid	Bid refers to make an offer at an auction or at a judicial sale.
Options	Options give the owner the right but not the obligation to buy or sell an underlying security at a set price for a given time period.
Broker	An agent who bargains or carries on negotiations in behalf of the principal as an intermediary between the latter and third persons in transacting business relative to the acquisition of contractual rights, or to the sale or purchase of property the custody of which is not entrusted to him or her for the purpose of discharging the agency is called a broker.
Mediation	Mediation consists of a process of alternative dispute resolution in which a (generally) neutral third party using appropriate techniques, assists two or more parties to help them negotiate an agreement, with concrete effects, on a matter of common interest.
Business process	Business process refers to the individual activities of an enterprise. Processes can be viewed at a high level, for example, 'marketing,' or at the level of detailed subprocesses, for example, 'customer retention.'.
Tangible	Having a physical existence is referred to as the tangible. Personal property other than real estate, such as cars, boats, stocks, or other assets.
Policy	Similar to a script in that a policy can be a less than completely rational decision-making method. Involves the use of a pre-existing set of decision steps for any problem that presents itself.
Customer service	The ability of logistics management to satisfy users in terms of time, dependability, communication, and convenience is called the customer service.
Inventory	Inventory refers to physical material purchased from suppliers, which may or may not be reworked for sale to customers. A unique element of services-the need for and cost of having a service provider available.
Automation	Automation allows machines to do work previously accomplished by people.

Go to **Cram101.com** for the Practice Tests for this Chapter.

Go to **Cram101.com** for the Practice Tests for this Chapter.
And, **NEVER** highlight a book again!

Competitive advantage	A business is said to have a competitive advantage when its unique strengths, often based on cost, quality, time, and innovation, offer consumers a greater percieved value and there by diffetiating it from its competitors.
Globalization	Trend away from distinct national economic units and toward one huge global market is called globalization. Globalization is caused by four fundamental forms of capital movement throughout the global economy.
Channel	Channel, in communications (sometimes called communications channel), refers to the medium used to convey information from a sender (or transmitter) to a receiver.
Restitution	A remedy whereby one is able to obtain the return of that which he has given the other party, or an amount of money equivalent to that which he has given the other party is referred to as restitution.
Cultural values	The values that employees need to have and act on for the organization to act on the strategic values are called cultural values.
Exchange	The trade of things of value between buyer and seller so that each is better off after the trade is called the exchange.
Conversion	Conversion refers to any distinct act of dominion wrongfully exerted over another's personal property in denial of or inconsistent with his rights therein. That tort committed by a person who deals with chattels not belonging to him in a manner that is inconsistent with the ownership of the lawful owner.
Refunding	The process of retiring an old bond issue before maturity and replacing it with a new issue is refunding. Refunding will occur when interest rates have fallen and new bonds may be sold at lower interest rates.
Margin	A deposit by a buyer in stocks with a seller or a stockbroker, as security to cover fluctuations in the market in reference to stocks that the buyer has purchased but for which he has not paid is a margin. Commodities are also traded on margin.
Target marketing	Marketing directed toward those groups an organization decides it can serve profitably is called target marketing.
Configuration	An organization's shape, which reflects the division of labor and the means of coordinating the divided tasks is configuration.
Bankruptcy	The state of a person who is unable to pay his or her debts without respect to time is called bankruptcy.
Holding	The holding is a court's determination of a matter of law based on the issue presented in the particular case. In other words: under this law, with these facts, this result.
Quality assurance	Those activities associated with assuring the quality of a product or service is called quality assurance.
Total Quality Management	The practice of striving for customer satisfaction by ensuring quality from all departments in an organization is called total quality management.
Quality management	Quality management is a method for ensuring that all the activities necessary to design, develop and implement a product or service are effective and efficient with respect to the system and its performance.
Compliance	A type of influence process where a receiver accepts the position advocated by a source to obtain favorable outcomes or to avoid punishment is the compliance.
Money management	Money management refers to managing a firm's global cash resources efficiently.
Licensing	Licensing is a form of strategic alliance which involves the sale of a right to use certain

Go to **Cram101.com** for the Practice Tests for this Chapter.
And, **NEVER** highlight a book again!

proprietary knowledge (so called intellectual property) in a defined way.

Grant	Grant refers to an intergovernmental transfer of funds . Since the New Deal, state and local governments have become increasingly dependent upon federal grants for an almost infinite variety of programs.
Acceptance	The actual or implied receipt and retention of that which is tendered or offered is the acceptance.
Niche marketing	Niche marketing refers to the process of finding small but profitable market segments and designing custom-made products for them.
Niche	In industry, a niche is a situation or an activity perfectly suited to a person. A niche can imply a working position or an area suited to a person who occupies it. Basically, a job where a person is able to succeed and thrive.
Innovation	The process of creating and doing new things that are introduced into the marketplace as products, processes, or services is innovation.
Communication	Communication refers to the social process in which two or more parties exchange information and share meaning.
Customer retention	Customer retention refers to the percentage of customers who return to a service provider or continue to purchase a manufactured product.
Customer contact	Customer contact refers to a characteristic of services that notes that customers tend to be more involved in the production of services than they are in manufactured goods.
Demographics	Demographics is a shorthand term for 'population characteristics'. Demographics include race, age, income, mobility (in terms of travel time to work or number of vehicles available), educational attainment, home ownership, employment status, and even location. Demographics are primarily used in economic and marketing research.
Demographic	A demographic is a term used in marketing and broadcasting, to describe a demographic grouping or a market segment.
Compensation	A payment that is given or recieved as reparation for a service or loss is referred to as compensation.
Marketing management	Marketing management refers to the process of planning and executing the conception, pricing, promotion, and distribution of ideas, goods, and services to create mutually beneficial exchanges.

Go to **Cram101.com** for the Practice Tests for this Chapter.

Go to **Cram101.com** for the Practice Tests for this Chapter.
And, **NEVER** highlight a book again!

Marketing	The American Marketing Association suggests that Marketing is "the process of planning and executing the pricing, promotion, and distribution of goods, ideas, and services to create exchanges that satisfy individual and organizational goals."
Evaluation	The consumer's appraisal of the product or brand on important attributes is called evaluation.
Manager	A person who is formally responsible for supporting the work efforts of other people is a manager.
Product	Any physical good, service, or idea that satisfies a want or need is called product. Product in project management is a physical entity created as a result of project work.
Advertising	Advertising refers to paid, nonpersonal communication through various media by organizations and individuals who are in some way identified in the advertising message.
Consumer behavior	Consumer behavior refers to the actions a person takes in purchasing and using products and services, including the mental and social processes that precede and follow these actions.
Consumer	A consumer is a individual or household that consume goods and services generated within the economy. Since this includes just about everyone, the term is a political term as much as an economic term when it is used in everyday speech.
Communication	Communication refers to the social process in which two or more parties exchange information and share meaning.
Acquisition	A company's purchase of the property and obligations of another company is an acquisition.
Options	Options give the owner the right but not the obligation to buy or sell an underlying security at a set price for a given time period.
External search	External search refers to the search process whereby consumers seek and acquire information from external sources such as advertising, other people, or public sources.
Preference	The act of a debtor in paying or securing one or more of his creditors in a manner more favorable to them than to other creditors or to the exclusion of such other creditors is a preference. In the absence of statute, a preference is perfectly good, but to be legal it must be bona fide, and not a mere subterfuge of the debtor to secure a future benefit to himself or to prevent the application of his property to his debts.
Evoked set	The group of brands that a consumer would consider acceptable from among all the brands in the product class of which he or she is aware is called evoked set.
Brand	A name, symbol, or design that identifies the goods or services of one seller or group of sellers and distinguishes them from the goods and services of competitors is a brand.
Decision rule	Decision rule refers to a statement that tells a decision maker which alternative to choose based on the characteristics of the decision situation.
Compensatory	Damages that will compensate a part for direct losses due to an injury suffered are referred to as compensatory .
Management	Management characterizes the process of leading and directing all or part of an organization, often a business, through the deployment and manipulation of resources. Early twentieth-century management writer Mary Parker Follett defined management as "the art of getting things done through people."
Competitor	Other organizations in the same industry or type of business that provide a good or service to the same set of customers is referred to as a competitor.
Cognitive dissonance	The anxiety a person experiences when he or she simultaneously possesses two sets of knowledge or perceptions that are contradictory or incongruent is referred to as the

Go to **Cram101.com** for the Practice Tests for this Chapter.

Go to **Cram101.com** for the Practice Tests for this Chapter.
And, **NEVER** highlight a book again!

	cognitive dissonance.
Promotion	Promotion refers to all the techniques sellers use to motivate people to buy products or services. An attempt by marketers to inform people about products and to persuade them to participate in an exchange.
Trustee	A person in whom property is vested in trust for another is called the trustee.
Users	Users refer to people in the organization who actually use the product or service purchased by the buying center.
Customer service	The ability of logistics management to satisfy users in terms of time, dependability, communication, and convenience is called the customer service.
Target marketing	Marketing directed toward those groups an organization decides it can serve profitably is called target marketing.
Corporation	A form of business organization that is owned by owners, called shareholders, who have no inherent right to manage the business, and is managed by a board of directors that is elected by the shareholders is called a corporation.
Competitive Strategy	An outline of how a business intends to compete with other firms in the same industry is called competitive strategy.
Principal	In agency law, one under whose direction an agent acts and for whose benefit that agent acts is a principal.
Perceived quality	A dimension of quality identified by David Garvin that refers to a subjective assessment of a product's quality based on criteria defined by the observer is a perceived quality.
Policy	Similar to a script in that a policy can be a less than completely rational decision-making method. Involves the use of a pre-existing set of decision steps for any problem that presents itself.
Perceived risk	The anxieties felt because the consumer cannot anticipate the outcomes of a purchase but believes that there may be negative consequences is called a perceived risk.
Purchasing	Purchasing refers to the function in a firm that searches for quality material resources, finds the best suppliers, and negotiates the best price for goods and services.
Financial risk	The risk related to the inability of the firm to meet its debt obligations as they come due is called financial risk.
Inseparability	Inseparability is a characteristic of services, which describes how service products tend to be produced at the same time as they are consumed.
Production	The creation of finished goods and services using the factors of production: land, labor, capital, entrepreneurship, and knowledge.
Economics	The study of how society chooses to employ resources to produce goods and services and distribute them for consumption among various competing groups and individuals is economics.
Intangibility	A unique element of services-services cannot be held, touched, or seen before the purchase decision which is referred to as intangibility.
Personnel	A collective term for all of the employees of an organization. Personnel is also commonly used to refer to the personnel management function or the organizational unit responsible for administering personnel programs.
Loyalty	Marketers tend to define customer loyalty as making repeat purchases. Some argue that it should be defined attitudinally as a strongly positive feeling about the brand.
Brand loyalty	The degree to which customers are satisfied, like the brand, and are committed to further

Go to **Cram101.com** for the Practice Tests for this Chapter.

Go to **Cram101.com** for the Practice Tests for this Chapter.
And, **NEVER** highlight a book again!

purchase is referred to as brand loyalty.

Incentive	A reward offered by a marketer to a prospective customer in return for furnishing information or making a purchase is referred to as an incentive.
Insurance	A means for persons and businesses to protect themselves against the risk of loss is insurance.
Consideration	Consideration in contract law, a basic requirement for an enforceable agreement under traditional contract principles, defined in this text as legal value, bargained for and given in exchange for an act or promise. In corporation law, cash or property contributed to a corporation in exchange for shares, or a promise to contribute such cash or property.
Mass media	Mass media refers to non-personal channels of communication that allow a message to be sent to many individuals at one time.
Complexity	The technical sophistication of the product and hence the amount of understanding required to use it is referred to as complexity. It is the opposite of simplicity.
Target market	One or more specific groups of potential consumers toward which an organization directs its marketing program are a target market.
Marketing mix	The marketing mix approach to marketing is a model of crafting and implementing marketing strategies. It stresses the "mixing" or blending of various factors in such a way that both organizational and consumer (target markets) objectives are attained.
Marketing Plan	Marketing plan refers to a road map for the marketing activities of an organization for a specified future period of time, such as one year or five years.
Bottom line	Bottom line refers to the last line in a profit and loss statement; it refers to net profit.
Distribution	Distribution is one of the four aspects of marketing. A distribution business is the middleman between the manufacturer and retailer or (usually)in commercial or industrial the business customer.
Diversification	Diversification is a strategy that takes the organization away from both its current markets and products, as opposed to either market or product development.
Product mix	The combination of product lines offered by a manufacturer is referred to as product mix.
Customer experience	The sum total of interactions that a customer has with a company's website is referred to as the customer experience.
Efficiency	Efficiency refers to the use of minimal resources, such as raw materials, money, and people-to produce a desired volume of output.
Exchange	The trade of things of value between buyer and seller so that each is better off after the trade is called the exchange.
Client	The organizations with the products, services, or causes to be marketed and for which advertising agencies and other marketing promotional firms provide services is referred to as a client.
Property	Property refers to something that is capable of being owned. A right or interest associated with something that gives the owner the ability to exercise dominion over it.
Contact personnel	The people at the 'front lines' who interact with the public in a service setting are contact personnel.
Discount	A discount is the reduction of the base price of a product.
Levy	At common law, a levy on goods consisted of an officer's entering the premises where they were and either leaving an assistant in charge of them or removing them after taking an

Go to **Cram101.com** for the Practice Tests for this Chapter.
And, **NEVER** highlight a book again!

inventory. Today, courts differ as to what is a valid levy, but by the weight of authority there must be an actual or constructive seizure of the goods. In most states, a levy on land must be made by some unequivocal act of the officer indicating the intention of singling out certain real estate for the satisfaction of the debt.

Retailing

All activities involved in selling, renting, and providing goods and services to ultimate consumers for personal, family, or household use is referred to as retailing.

Go to **Cram101.com** for the Practice Tests for this Chapter.

Go to **Cram101.com** for the Practice Tests for this Chapter.
And, **NEVER** highlight a book again!

Marketing	The American Marketing Association suggests that Marketing is "the process of planning and executing the pricing, promotion, and distribution of goods, ideas, and services to create exchanges that satisfy individual and organizational goals."
Business ethics	The study of what makes up good and bad conduct as related to business activities and values is business ethics.
Controlling	A management function that involves determining whether or not an organization is progressing toward its goals and objectives, and taking corrective action if it is not is called controlling.
Exchange	The trade of things of value between buyer and seller so that each is better off after the trade is called the exchange.
Bail	Bail refers to an amount of money the defendant pays to the court upon release from custody as security that he or she will return for trial.
White-collar crime	A crime committed in a commercial context by a member of the professional-managerial class is referred to as a white-collar crime.
Intangibility	A unique element of services-services cannot be held, touched, or seen before the purchase decision which is referred to as intangibility.
Inseparability	Inseparability is a characteristic of services, which describes how service products tend to be produced at the same time as they are consumed.
Preventive maintenance	Maintaining scheduled upkeep and improvement to equipment so equipment can actually improve with age is called the preventive maintenance.
Personnel	A collective term for all of the employees of an organization. Personnel is also commonly used to refer to the personnel management function or the organizational unit responsible for administering personnel programs.
Management	Management characterizes the process of leading and directing all or part of an organization, often a business, through the deployment and manipulation of resources. Early twentieth-century management writer Mary Parker Follett defined management as "the art of getting things done through people."
Incentive	A reward offered by a marketer to a prospective customer in return for furnishing information or making a purchase is referred to as an incentive.
Looting	In corporation law, the transfer of a corporation's assets to its managers or controlling shareholders at less than fair value is referred to as looting.
Quality control	The measurement of products and services against set standards is referred to as quality control.
Evaluation	The consumer's appraisal of the product or brand on important attributes is called evaluation.
Production	The creation of finished goods and services using the factors of production: land, labor, capital, entrepreneurship, and knowledge.
Purchasing	Purchasing refers to the function in a firm that searches for quality material resources, finds the best suppliers, and negotiates the best price for goods and services.
Venture capital	Venture capital is capital provided by outside investors for financing of new, growing or struggling businesses. Venture capital investments generally are high risk investments but offer the potential for above average returns.
Capital	Contributions of money and other property to a business made by the owners of the business are capital.

Go to **Cram101.com** for the Practice Tests for this Chapter.
And, **NEVER** highlight a book again!

Stock	In financial terminology, stock is the capital raized by a corporation, through the issuance and sale of shares. A shareholder is any person or organization which owns one or more shares of a corporation's stock. The aggregate value of a corporation's issued shares is its market capitalization.
Accounting	The recording, classifying, summarizing, and interpreting of financial events and transactions to provide management and other interested parties the information they need to make good decisions is called accounting.
Revenue	Revenue refers to the total amount of money a business earns in a given period by selling goods and services. The value of what is received for goods sold, services rendered.
Property	Property refers to something that is capable of being owned. A right or interest associated with something that gives the owner the ability to exercise dominion over it.
Advertising	Advertising refers to paid, nonpersonal communication through various media by organizations and individuals who are in some way identified in the advertising message.
Barter	Barter refers to the trading of goods and services for other goods and services directly.
Discount	A discount is the reduction of the base price of a product.
Coupon	In finance, a coupon is "attached" to bonds, either physically (as with old bonds) or electronically. Each coupon represents a predetermined payment promized to the bond-holder in return for his or her loan of money to the bond-issuer. The bond-holder is typically not the original lender, but receives this payment for effectively lending the money. The coupon rate (the amount promized per dollar of the face value of the bond) helps determine the interest rate or yield on the bond.
Expense	An expense refers to costs involved in operating a business, such as rent, utilities, and salaries.
Bid	Bid refers to make an offer at an auction or at a judicial sale.
Broker	An agent who bargains or carries on negotiations in behalf of the principal as an intermediary between the latter and third persons in transacting business relative to the acquisition of contractual rights, or to the sale or purchase of property the custody of which is not entrusted to him or her for the purpose of discharging the agency is called a broker.
Industry	Industry refers to a group of firms offering products that are close substitutes for each other.
Insurance	A means for persons and businesses to protect themselves against the risk of loss is insurance.
Options	Options give the owner the right but not the obligation to buy or sell an underlying security at a set price for a given time period.
Bottom line	Bottom line refers to the last line in a profit and loss statement; it refers to net profit.
Acceptance	The actual or implied receipt and retention of that which is tendered or offered is the acceptance.
Participation	Participation refers to the process of giving employees a voice in making decisions about their own work.
Beneficiary	The person for whose benefit an insurance policy, trust, will, or contract is established is a beneficiary. In the case of a contract, the beneficiary is called a third-party beneficiary.
Promotion	Promotion refers to all the techniques sellers use to motivate people to buy products or

Go to **Cram101.com** for the Practice Tests for this Chapter.

Go to **Cram101.com** for the Practice Tests for this Chapter.
And, **NEVER** highlight a book again!

	services. An attempt by marketers to inform people about products and to persuade them to participate in an exchange.
Remainder	A remainder in property law is a future interest created in a transferee that is capable of becoming possessory upon the natural termination of a prior estate created by the same instrument.
Product	Any physical good, service, or idea that satisfies a want or need is called product. Product in project management is a physical entity created as a result of project work.
Utilitarianism	A personal moral philosophy that focuses on the 'greatest good for the greatest number' by assessing the costs and benefits of the consequences of ethical behavior is referred to as utilitarianism.
Customer service	The ability of logistics management to satisfy users in terms of time, dependability, communication, and convenience is called the customer service.
Manager	A person who is formally responsible for supporting the work efforts of other people is a manager.
Conflict of interest	A conflict that occurs when a corporate officer or director enters into a transaction with the corporation in which he or she has a personal interest is a conflict of interest.
Interest	Interest refers to the payment the issuer of the bond makes to the bondholders for use of the borrowed money. It is the return to capital achieved over time or as the result of an event.
Product liability	Part of tort law that holds businesses liable for harm that results from the production, design, sale, or use of products they market is referred to as product liability.
Liability	A liability is anything that is a hindrance, or puts individuals at a disadvantage.
Capitalism	An economic system in which all or most of the factors of production and distribution are privately owned and operated for profit is called capitalism.
Contribution	In business organization law, the cash or property contributed to a business by its owners is referred to as contribution.
Asset	In business and accounting an asset is anything owned which can produce future economic benefit, whether in possession or by right to take possession, by a person or a group acting together, e.g. a company, the measurement of which can be expressed in monetary terms. Asset is listed on the balance sheet. It has a normal balance of debit.
Closing	The finalization of a real estate sales transaction that passes title to the property from the seller to the buyer is referred to as a closing. Closing is a sales term which refers to the process of making a sale. It refers to reaching the final step, which may be an exchange of money or acquiring a signature.
Competitor	Other organizations in the same industry or type of business that provide a good or service to the same set of customers is referred to as a competitor.
Premium	Premium refers to the fee charged by an insurance company for an insurance policy. The rate of losses must be relatively predictable: In order to set the premium (prices) insurers must be able to estimate them accurately.
Content	Content refers to all digital information included on a website, including the presentation form-text, video, audio, and graphics.
Insider trading	A form of investment in which insiders use private company information to further their own fortunes or those of their family and friends is called insider trading.
Takeover	A takeover in business refers to one company (the acquirer) purchasing another (the target). Such events resemble mergers, but without the formation of a new company.

Go to **Cram101.com** for the Practice Tests for this Chapter.
And, **NEVER** highlight a book again!

Undue influence	Undue influence is an equitable doctrine that involves one person taking advantage of a position of power over another person.
Client	The organizations with the products, services, or causes to be marketed and for which advertising agencies and other marketing promotional firms provide services is referred to as a client.
Equity	Equity is the name given to the set of legal principles, in countries following the English common law tradition, which supplement strict rules of law where their application would operate harshly, so as to achieve what is sometimes referred to as "natural justice."
Communication	Communication refers to the social process in which two or more parties exchange information and share meaning.
Mistake	In contract law a mistake is incorrect understanding by one or more parties to a contract and may be used as grounds to invalidate the agreement. Common law has identified three different types of mistake in contract: unilateral mistake, mutual mistake, and common mistake.
Authority	Authority in agency law, refers to an agent's ability to affect his principal's legal relations with third parties. Also used to refer to an actor's legal power or ability to do something. In addition, sometimes used to refer to a statute, case, or other legal source that justifies a particular result.
Contract	A contract is a "promise" or an "agreement" that is enforced or recognized by the law. In the civil law, contracts are considered to be part of the general law of obligations. This article describes the law relating to contracts in common law jurisdictions.
Utility	An economic term that refers to the value or want-satisfying ability that's added to goods or services by organizations when the products are made more useful or accessible to consumers than before is a utility.
Corporate culture	The whole collection of beliefs, values, and behaviors of a firm that send messages to those within and outside the company about how business is done is the corporate culture.
Organizational structure	Refers to how a company is put together and reflects some of the underlying ways that people interact with one another in and across jobs or departments is referred to as organizational structure.
Hierarchy	A system of grouping people in an organization according to rank from the top down in which all subordinate managers must report to one person is called a hierarchy.
Control system	A control system is a device or set of devices that manage the behavior of other devices. Some devices or systems are not controllable.A control system is an interconnection of components connected or related in such a manner as to command, direct, or regulate itself or another system.
Relationship marketing	Marketing whose goal is to keep individual customers over time by offering them products that exactly meet their requirements is called relationship marketing.
Compromise	Compromise occurs when the interaction is moderately important to meeting goals and the goals are neither completely compatible nor completely incompatible.
Corporate goals	Strategic performance targets that the entire organization must reach to pursue its vision are referred to as corporate goals.
Social responsibility	Social responsibility is a doctrine that claims that an entity whether it is state, government, corporation, organization or individual has a responsibility to society.
Publicity	Publicity refers to any information about an individual, product, or organization that's distributed to the public through the media and that's not paid for or controlled by the seller.

Go to **Cram101.com** for the Practice Tests for this Chapter.

Go to **Cram101.com** for the Practice Tests for this Chapter.
And, **NEVER** highlight a book again!

Trust	Trust refers to a legal relationship in which a person who has legal title to property has the duty to hold it for the use or benefit of another person. The term is also used in a general sense to mean confidence reposed in one person by another.
Employee orientation	Employee orientation refers to the activity that introduces new employees to the organization; to fellow employees; to their immediate supervisors; and to the policies, practices, and objectives of the firm.
Appeal	Appeal refers to the act of asking an appellate court to overturn a decision after the trial court's final judgment has been entered.
Code of ethics	A formal statement of ethical principles and rules of conduct is a code of ethics. Some may have the force of law; these are often promulgated by the (quasi-)governmental agency responsible for licensing a profession. Violations of these codes may be subject to administrative (e.g., loss of license), civil or penal remedies.
Loyalty	Marketers tend to define customer loyalty as making repeat purchases. Some argue that it should be defined attitudinally as a strongly positive feeling about the brand.
International Business	International business refers to any firm that engages in international trade or investment.
Marketing research	Marketing research refers to the analysis of markets to determine opportunities and challenges, and to find the information needed to make good decisions.
Personal selling	Personal selling is interpersonal communication, often face to face, between a sales representative and an individual or group, usually with the objective of making a sale.
Sales management	Planning the selling program and implementing and controlling the personal selling effort of the firm is called sales management.
Direct marketing	Promotional element that uses direct communication with consumers to generate a response in the form of an order, a request for further information, or a visit to a retail outlet is direct marketing.
Database marketing	The use of specific information about individual customers and/or prospects to implement more effective and efficient marketing communications is called database marketing.
Marketing strategy	Marketing strategy refers to the means by which a marketing goal is to be achieved, usually characterized by a specified target market and a marketing program to reach it.
Administration	Administration refers to the management and direction of the affairs of governments and institutions; a collective term for all policymaking officials of a government; the execution and implementation of public policy.

Go to **Cram101.com** for the Practice Tests for this Chapter.

Go to **Cram101.com** for the Practice Tests for this Chapter.
And, **NEVER** highlight a book again!

Production	The creation of finished goods and services using the factors of production: land, labor, capital, entrepreneurship, and knowledge.
Marketing mix	The marketing mix approach to marketing is a model of crafting and implementing marketing strategies. It stresses the "mixing" or blending of various factors in such a way that both organizational and consumer (target markets) objectives are attained.
Marketing	The American Marketing Association suggests that Marketing is "the process of planning and executing the pricing, promotion, and distribution of goods, ideas, and services to create exchanges that satisfy individual and organizational goals."
Promotion	Promotion refers to all the techniques sellers use to motivate people to buy products or services. An attempt by marketers to inform people about products and to persuade them to participate in an exchange.
Efficiency	Efficiency refers to the use of minimal resources, such as raw materials, money, and people- to produce a desired volume of output.
Distribution center	Designed to facilitate the timely movement of goods and represent a very important part of a supply chain is a distribution center.
Distribution	Distribution is one of the four aspects of marketing. A distribution business is the middleman between the manufacturer and retailer or (usually)in commercial or industrial the business customer.
Benchmarking	Discovering how others do something better than your own firm so you can imitate or leapfrog competition is called benchmarking.
Warehouse	Warehouse refers to a location, often decentralized, that a firm uses to store, consolidate, age, or mix stock; house product-recall programs; or ease tax burdens.
Options	Options give the owner the right but not the obligation to buy or sell an underlying security at a set price for a given time period.
Competitive Strategy	An outline of how a business intends to compete with other firms in the same industry is called competitive strategy.
Personnel	A collective term for all of the employees of an organization. Personnel is also commonly used to refer to the personnel management function or the organizational unit responsible for administering personnel programs.
Management	Management characterizes the process of leading and directing all or part of an organization, often a business, through the deployment and manipulation of resources. Early twentieth-century management writer Mary Parker Follett defined management as "the art of getting things done through people."
Minimum wage	Minimum wage refers to the lowest amount that employers are legally allowed to pay; the 1990 amendment of the Fair Labor Standards Act permits a subminimum wage to workers under the age of 20 for a period of up to 90 days.
Competition	In business, competition occurs when rival organizations with similar products and services attempt to gain customers.
Controlling	A management function that involves determining whether or not an organization is progressing toward its goals and objectives, and taking corrective action if it is not is called controlling.
Complexity	The technical sophistication of the product and hence the amount of understanding required to use it is referred to as complexity. It is the opposite of simplicity.
Competitor	Other organizations in the same industry or type of business that provide a good or service

Go to **Cram101.com** for the Practice Tests for this Chapter.

Go to **Cram101.com** for the Practice Tests for this Chapter.
And, **NEVER** highlight a book again!

	to the same set of customers is referred to as a competitor.
Mentoring	Mentoring refers to a developmental relationship between a more experienced mentor and a less experienced partner referred to as a mentee or protégé. Usually - but not necessarily - the mentor/protégé pair will be of the same sex.
Mentor	An experienced employee who supervises, coaches, and guides lower-level employees by introducing them to the right people and generally being their organizational sponsor is a mentor.
Operations management	A specialized area in management that converts or transforms resources into goods and services is operations management.
Customer service	The ability of logistics management to satisfy users in terms of time, dependability, communication, and convenience is called the customer service.
Capacity planning	The determination and adjustment of the organization's ability to produce products and services to match customer demand is called capacity planning.
Product	Any physical good, service, or idea that satisfies a want or need is called product. Product in project management is a physical entity created as a result of project work.
Copyright	Copyright refers to a set of exclusive rights, protected by federal law, pertaining to certain creative works such as books, musical compositions, computer programs, works of art, and so forth. The rights are to reproduce the work in question, to prepare derivative works based on it, to sell or otherwise distribute it, and to perform or display it publicly.
Participation	Participation refers to the process of giving employees a voice in making decisions about their own work.
Consumer behavior	Consumer behavior refers to the actions a person takes in purchasing and using products and services, including the mental and social processes that precede and follow these actions.
Consumer	A consumer is a individual or household that consume goods and services generated within the economy. Since this includes just about everyone, the term is a political term as much as an economic term when it is used in everyday speech.
Inventory	Inventory refers to physical material purchased from suppliers, which may or may not be reworked for sale to customers. A unique element of services-the need for and cost of having a service provider available.
Logo	Logo refers to device or other brand name that cannot be spoken.
Product mix	The combination of product lines offered by a manufacturer is referred to as product mix.
Contact personnel	The people at the 'front lines' who interact with the public in a service setting are contact personnel.
Compromise	Compromise occurs when the interaction is moderately important to meeting goals and the goals are neither completely compatible nor completely incompatible.
Manager	A person who is formally responsible for supporting the work efforts of other people is a manager.
Yield	The interest rate that equates a future value or an annuity to a given present value is a yield.
Product line	A group of products that are physically similar or are intended for a similar market are called the product line.
Exhibit	Exhibit refers to a copy of a written instrument on which a pleading is founded, annexed to the pleading and by reference made a part of it. Any paper or thing offered in evidence and

Go to Cram101.com for the Practice Tests for this Chapter.

Go to **Cram101.com** for the Practice Tests for this Chapter.
And, **NEVER** highlight a book again!

marked for identification.

Utility	An economic term that refers to the value or want-satisfying ability that's added to goods or services by organizations when the products are made more useful or accessible to consumers than before is a utility.
Competitive advantage	A business is said to have a competitive advantage when its unique strengths, often based on cost, quality, time, and innovation, offer consumers a greater percieved value and there by differtiating it from its competitors.
Customer contact	Customer contact refers to a characteristic of services that notes that customers tend to be more involved in the production of services than they are in manufactured goods.
Core	A core is the set of feasible allocations in an economy that cannot be improved upon by subset of the set of the economy's consumers (a coalition).
Argument	The discussion by counsel for the respective parties of their contentions on the law and the facts of the case being tried in order to aid the jury in arriving at a correct and just conclusion is called argument.
Capital	Contributions of money and other property to a business made by the owners of the business are capital.
Purchasing	Purchasing refers to the function in a firm that searches for quality material resources, finds the best suppliers, and negotiates the best price for goods and services.
Interest	Interest refers to the payment the issuer of the bond makes to the bondholders for use of the borrowed money. It is the return to capital achieved over time or as the result of an event.
Franchise	A business established or operated under an authorization to sell or distribute a company's goods or services in a particular area is a franchise.
Advertising	Advertising refers to paid, nonpersonal communication through various media by organizations and individuals who are in some way identified in the advertising message.
Remainder	A remainder in property law is a future interest created in a transferee that is capable of becoming possessory upon the natural termination of a prior estate created by the same instrument.
Industry	Industry refers to a group of firms offering products that are close substitutes for each other.
Hierarchy	A system of grouping people in an organization according to rank from the top down in which all subordinate managers must report to one person is called a hierarchy.
Loyalty	Marketers tend to define customer loyalty as making repeat purchases. Some argue that it should be defined attitudinally as a strongly positive feeling about the brand.
Empowerment	Giving employees the authority and responsibility to respond quickly to customer requests is called empowerment.
Performance management	The means through which managers ensure that employees' activities and outputs are congruent with the organization's goals is referred to as performance management.
Restructuring	Restructuring is the corporate management term for the act of partially dismantling and reorganizing a company for the purpose of making it more efficient and therefore more profitable.
Personalization	The consumer-initiated practice of generating content on a marketer's website that is custom tailored to an individual's specific needs and preferences is called personalization.
Discount	A discount is the reduction of the base price of a product.

Go to **Cram101.com** for the Practice Tests for this Chapter.
And, **NEVER** highlight a book again!

Flowchart	A pictorial representation of the progression of a particular process over time is called a flowchart. They are commonly used in business/economic presentations to help the audience visualize the content better, or to find flaws in the process
Accounting	The recording, classifying, summarizing, and interpreting of financial events and transactions to provide management and other interested parties the information they need to make good decisions is called accounting.
Layout	Layout refers to the physical arrangement of the various parts of an advertisement including the headline, subheads, illustrations, body copy, and any identifying marks.
Bottom line	Bottom line refers to the last line in a profit and loss statement; it refers to net profit.
Buyer	A buyer refers to a role in the buying center with formal authority and responsibility to select the supplier and negotiate the terms of the contract.
Users	Users refer to people in the organization who actually use the product or service purchased by the buying center.
Intangibility	A unique element of services-services cannot be held, touched, or seen before the purchase decision which is referred to as intangibility.
E-commerce	The sale of goods and services by computer over the Internet is referred to as the e-commerce.
Beta test	A process, most often used in B2B markets, in which customers are identified who are willing to use an early version of a product and provide feedback to the producer before the product is made available for sale is a beta test.
Level of service	The degree of service provided to the customer by self, limited, and full-service retailers is referred to as the level of service.
Collateral	Collateral is any asset, property, stock, etc., put up to secure the performance of a promise, so that if the promisor fails to meet that promise, the creditor may look to the asset to make him whole.
Tangible	Having a physical existence is referred to as the tangible. Personal property other than real estate, such as cars, boats, stocks, or other assets.
Agent	One who acts under the direction of a principal for the principal's benefit in a legal relationship known as agency is called agent.
Property	Property refers to something that is capable of being owned. A right or interest associated with something that gives the owner the ability to exercise dominion over it.
Mistake	In contract law a mistake is incorrect understanding by one or more parties to a contract and may be used as grounds to invalidate the agreement. Common law has identified three different types of mistake in contract: unilateral mistake, mutual mistake, and common mistake.
Visibility	Visibility is used in marketing, as a measure of how much the public sees a product or its advertising.
Positioning	The art and science of fitting the product or service to one or more segments of the market in such a way as to set it meaningfully apart from competition is called positioning.
Structural change	Any change in the way in which an organization is designed and managed is referred to as a structural change.
Unbundling	Relying on more than one financial technique to transfer funds across borders is called unbundling.
Penetration	Strategy in which a product is priced low to attract many customers and discourage

Go to **Cram101.com** for the Practice Tests for this Chapter.

Go to **Cram101.com** for the Practice Tests for this Chapter.
And, **NEVER** highlight a book again!

strategy	competition is referred to as penetration strategy.
Public administration	Whatever governments do, for good or ill, is referred to as public administration. It is public administration's political context that makes it public, that distinguishes it from private or business administration.
Administration	Administration refers to the management and direction of the affairs of governments and institutions; a collective term for all policymaking officials of a government; the execution and implementation of public policy.
Retailing	All activities involved in selling, renting, and providing goods and services to ultimate consumers for personal, family, or household use is referred to as retailing.
Audit	Audit refers to the verification of a company's books and records pursuant to federal securities laws, state laws, and stock exchange rules that must be performed by an independent CPA.

Go to **Cram101.com** for the Practice Tests for this Chapter.
And, **NEVER** highlight a book again!

Product	Any physical good, service, or idea that satisfies a want or need is called product. Product in project management is a physical entity created as a result of project work.
Efficiency	Efficiency refers to the use of minimal resources, such as raw materials, money, and people- to produce a desired volume of output.
Marketing mix	The marketing mix approach to marketing is a model of crafting and implementing marketing strategies. It stresses the "mixing" or blending of various factors in such a way that both organizational and consumer (target markets) objectives are attained.
Marketing	The American Marketing Association suggests that Marketing is "the process of planning and executing the pricing, promotion, and distribution of goods, ideas, and services to create exchanges that satisfy individual and organizational goals."
Policy	Similar to a script in that a policy can be a less than completely rational decision-making method. Involves the use of a pre-existing set of decision steps for any problem that presents itself.
Management	Management characterizes the process of leading and directing all or part of an organization, often a business, through the deployment and manipulation of resources. Early twentieth-century management writer Mary Parker Follett defined management as "the art of getting things done through people."
Production	The creation of finished goods and services using the factors of production: land, labor, capital, entrepreneurship, and knowledge.
Industrial goods	Components produced for use in the production of other products are called industrial goods.
Manager	A person who is formally responsible for supporting the work efforts of other people is a manager.
Customer value	Customer value refers to the unique combination of benefits received by targeted buyers that includes quality, price, convenience, on-time delivery, and both before-sale and after-sale service.
Personnel	A collective term for all of the employees of an organization. Personnel is also commonly used to refer to the personnel management function or the organizational unit responsible for administering personnel programs.
Receiver	A person that is appointed as a custodian of other people's property by a court of law or a creditor of the owner, pending a lawsuit or reorganization is called a receiver.
Marketing management	Marketing management refers to the process of planning and executing the conception, pricing, promotion, and distribution of ideas, goods, and services to create mutually beneficial exchanges.
Competitor	Other organizations in the same industry or type of business that provide a good or service to the same set of customers is referred to as a competitor.
Warranty	A warranty is a promise that something sold is as factually stated or legally implied by the seller. A warranty may be express or implied. A breach of warranty occurs when the promise is broken, i.e., a product is defective or not as should be expected by a reasonable buyer.
Buyer	A buyer refers to a role in the buying center with formal authority and responsibility to select the supplier and negotiate the terms of the contract.
Exchange	The trade of things of value between buyer and seller so that each is better off after the trade is called the exchange.
Content	Content refers to all digital information included on a website, including the presentation form-text, video, audio, and graphics.

Go to **Cram101.com** for the Practice Tests for this Chapter.

Go to **Cram101.com** for the Practice Tests for this Chapter.
And, **NEVER** highlight a book again!

Perceived risk	The anxieties felt because the consumer cannot anticipate the outcomes of a purchase but believes that there may be negative consequences is called a perceived risk.
Intangibility	A unique element of services-services cannot be held, touched, or seen before the purchase decision which is referred to as intangibility.
Inseparability	Inseparability is a characteristic of services, which describes how service products tend to be produced at the same time as they are consumed.
Inventory	Inventory refers to physical material purchased from suppliers, which may or may not be reworked for sale to customers. A unique element of services-the need for and cost of having a service provider available.
Fixed cost	Fixed cost refers to the sum of expenses of the firm that are stable and do not change with the quantity of product that is produced and sold.
Variable cost	The sum of the expenses of the firm that vary directly with the quantity of product that is produced and sold is called variable cost.
Discount	A discount is the reduction of the base price of a product.
Purchasing	Purchasing refers to the function in a firm that searches for quality material resources, finds the best suppliers, and negotiates the best price for goods and services.
Total cost	The total expense incurred by a firm in producing and marketing a product is the total cost. Total cost is the sum of fixed cost and variable cost. In physical distribution decisions, the sum of all applicable costs for logistical activities.
Industry	Industry refers to a group of firms offering products that are close substitutes for each other.
Expense	An expense refers to costs involved in operating a business, such as rent, utilities, and salaries.
Revenue	Revenue refers to the total amount of money a business earns in a given period by selling goods and services. The value of what is received for goods sold, services rendered.
Price discrimination	Price discrimination refers to the practice of charging different prices to different buyers for goods of like trade and quality. The Clayton Act as amended by the Robinson-Patman Act prohibits this action.
Options	Options give the owner the right but not the obligation to buy or sell an underlying security at a set price for a given time period.
Impossibility	A doctrine under which a party to a contract is relieved of his or her duty to perform when that performance has become impossible because of the occurrence of an event unforeseen at the time of contracting is referred to as impossibility.
Reverse auction	A buyer communicates a need for a product or service and would-be suppliers are invited to bid in competition with each other is a reverse auction.
Auction	A preexisting business model that operates successfully on the Internet by announcing an item for sale and permitting multiple purchasers to bid on them under specified rules and condition is an auction.
Bid	Bid refers to make an offer at an auction or at a judicial sale.
Users	Users refer to people in the organization who actually use the product or service purchased by the buying center.
Commerce	Commerce is the exchange of something of value between two entities. It is the central mechanism from which capitalism is derived.

Go to **Cram101.com** for the Practice Tests for this Chapter.

Go to **Cram101.com** for the Practice Tests for this Chapter.
And, **NEVER** highlight a book again!

Retailing	All activities involved in selling, renting, and providing goods and services to ultimate consumers for personal, family, or household use is referred to as retailing.
Market segments	Market segments refer to the groups that result from the process of market segmentation; these groups ideally have common needs and will respond similarly to a marketing action.
Family life cycle	Family life cycle refers to concept that demonstrates changing purchasing behavior as a person or a family matures.
Generation y	Generation y refers to Americans born after 1976, the year that many baby boomers began having children.
Coupon	In finance, a coupon is "attached" to bonds, either physically (as with old bonds) or electronically. Each coupon represents a predetermined payment promized to the bond-holder in return for his or her loan of money to the bond-issuer. The bond-holder is typically not the original lender, but receives this payment for effectively lending the money. The coupon rate (the amount promized per dollar of the face value of the bond) helps determine the interest rate or yield on the bond.
Promotion	Promotion refers to all the techniques sellers use to motivate people to buy products or services. An attempt by marketers to inform people about products and to persuade them to participate in an exchange.
Advertising	Advertising refers to paid, nonpersonal communication through various media by organizations and individuals who are in some way identified in the advertising message.
Evaluation	The consumer's appraisal of the product or brand on important attributes is called evaluation.
Cost of goods sold	A measure of the cost of merchandise sold or cost of raw materials and supplies used for producing items for resale is called cost of goods sold.
Accounting	The recording, classifying, summarizing, and interpreting of financial events and transactions to provide management and other interested parties the information they need to make good decisions is called accounting.
Depreciation	The systematic write-off of the cost of a tangible asset over its estimated useful life is called depreciation.
Activity-based costing	A control system that identifies the various activities needed to provide a product and allocates costs accordingly is an activity-based costing.
Vendor	A person who sells property to a vendee is a vendor. The words vendor and vendee are more commonly applied to the seller and purchaser of real estate, and the words seller and buyer are more commonly applied to the seller and purchaser of personal property.
Insurance	A means for persons and businesses to protect themselves against the risk of loss is insurance.
Economies of scale	A decline in costs with accumulated sales or production is an economies of scale. In advertising, economies of scale often occur in media purchases as the relative costs of advertising time and/or space may decline as the size of the media budget increases.
Perceived quality	A dimension of quality identified by David Garvin that refers to a subjective assessment of a product's quality based on criteria defined by the observer is a perceived quality.
Consideration	Consideration in contract law, a basic requirement for an enforceable agreement under traditional contract principles, defined in this text as legal value, bargained for and given in exchange for an act or promise. In corporation law, cash or property contributed to a corporation in exchange for shares, or a promise to contribute such cash or property.

Go to **Cram101.com** for the Practice Tests for this Chapter.

Go to **Cram101.com** for the Practice Tests for this Chapter.
And, **NEVER** highlight a book again!

Strategic alliance	Strategic alliance refers to a long-term partnership between two or more companies established to help each company build competitive market advantages.
Context	The effect of the background under which a message often takes on more and richer meaning is a context. Context is especially important in cross-cultural interactions because some cultures are said to be high context or low context.
Competition	In business, competition occurs when rival organizations with similar products and services attempt to gain customers.
Forward buying	Forward buying refers to a response to discounts offered by manufacturers in which retailers purchase more merchandise than they plan to sell during the promotion. The remaining stock is sold at a regular price later, or diverted to another store.
Estate	An estate is the totality of the legal rights, interests, entitlements and obligations attaching to property. In the context of wills and probate, it refers to the totality of the property which the deceased owned or in which some interest was held.
Contract	A contract is a "promise" or an "agreement" that is enforced or recognized by the law. In the civil law, contracts are considered to be part of the general law of obligations. This article describes the law relating to contracts in common law jurisdictions.
Agent	One who acts under the direction of a principal for the principal's benefit in a legal relationship known as agency is called agent.
Alienation	The voluntary act or acts by which one-person transfers his or her own property to another is referred to as alienation.
Price lining	Setting the price of line products at a limited number of different specific pricing points is referred to as price lining.
Trust	Trust refers to a legal relationship in which a person who has legal title to property has the duty to hold it for the use or benefit of another person. The term is also used in a general sense to mean confidence reposed in one person by another.
Penetration pricing	Penetration pricing refers to setting a low initial price on a new product to appeal immediately to the mass market.
Pricing	Pricing is the manual or automatic process of applying prices to purchase and sales orders, based on factors such as: a fixed amount, quantity break, promotion or sales campaign, specific vendor quote, price prevailing on entry, shipment or invoice date, combination of multiple orders or lines, and many others.
Premium	Premium refers to the fee charged by an insurance company for an insurance policy. The rate of losses must be relatively predictable: In order to set the premium (prices) insurers must be able to estimate them accurately.
Health insurance	Health insurance is a type of insurance whereby the insurer pays the medical costs of the insured if the insured becomes sick due to covered causes, or due to accidents. The insurer may be a private organization or a government agency.
Compromise	Compromise occurs when the interaction is moderately important to meeting goals and the goals are neither completely compatible nor completely incompatible.
Appeal	Appeal refers to the act of asking an appellate court to overturn a decision after the trial court's final judgment has been entered.
Bond	A long-term debt security that is secured by collateral is called a bond.
Certificates of deposit	Certificates of deposit refer to a certificate offered by banks, savings and loans, and other financial institutions for the deposit of funds at a given interest rate over a specified

Go to **Cram101.com** for the Practice Tests for this Chapter.
And, **NEVER** highlight a book again!

time period.

Incentive	A reward offered by a marketer to a prospective customer in return for furnishing information or making a purchase is referred to as an incentive.
Client	The organizations with the products, services, or causes to be marketed and for which advertising agencies and other marketing promotional firms provide services is referred to as a client.
Argument	The discussion by counsel for the respective parties of their contentions on the law and the facts of the case being tried in order to aid the jury in arriving at a correct and just conclusion is called argument.
Credibility	The extent to which a source is perceived as having knowledge, skill, or experience relevant to a communication topic and can be trusted to give an unbiased opinion or present objective information on the issue is called credibility.
Competitive advantage	A business is said to have a competitive advantage when its unique strengths, often based on cost, quality, time, and innovation, offer consumers a greater percieved value and there by differtiating it from its competitors.
Customer retention	Customer retention refers to the percentage of customers who return to a service provider or continue to purchase a manufactured product.
Tactic	A short-term immediate decision that, in its totality, leads to the achievement of strategic goals is called a tactic.
International Business	International business refers to any firm that engages in international trade or investment.
Marketing research	Marketing research refers to the analysis of markets to determine opportunities and challenges, and to find the information needed to make good decisions.
Best practice	In business management, a best practice is a generally accepted "best way of doing a thing". A best practice is formulated after the study of specific business or organizational case studies to determine the most broadly effective and efficient means of organizing a system or performing a function.

Go to **Cram101.com** for the Practice Tests for this Chapter.
And, **NEVER** highlight a book again!

Communication	Communication refers to the social process in which two or more parties exchange information and share meaning.
Marketing	The American Marketing Association suggests that Marketing is "the process of planning and executing the pricing, promotion, and distribution of goods, ideas, and services to create exchanges that satisfy individual and organizational goals."
Advertising	Advertising refers to paid, nonpersonal communication through various media by organizations and individuals who are in some way identified in the advertising message.
Evoked set	The group of brands that a consumer would consider acceptable from among all the brands in the product class of which he or she is aware is called evoked set.
Product	Any physical good, service, or idea that satisfies a want or need is called product. Product in project management is a physical entity created as a result of project work.
Users	Users refer to people in the organization who actually use the product or service purchased by the buying center.
Compatibility	Compatibility refers to used to describe a product characteristic, it means a good fit with other products used by the consumer or with the consumer's lifestyle. Used in a technical context, it means the ability of systems to work together.
Positioning	The art and science of fitting the product or service to one or more segments of the market in such a way as to set it meaningfully apart from competition is called positioning.
Target market	One or more specific groups of potential consumers toward which an organization directs its marketing program are a target market.
Competitor	Other organizations in the same industry or type of business that provide a good or service to the same set of customers is referred to as a competitor.
Markup	Markup is a term used in marketing to indicate how much the price of a product is above the cost of producing and distributing the product.
Conformance	A dimension of quality that refers to the extent to which a product lies within an allowable range of deviation from its specification is called the conformance.
Public relations	Public relations refers to the management function that evaluates public attitudes, changes policies and procedures in response to the public's requests, and executes a program of action and information to earn public understanding and acceptance.
Promotion	Promotion refers to all the techniques sellers use to motivate people to buy products or services. An attempt by marketers to inform people about products and to persuade them to participate in an exchange.
Marketing management	Marketing management refers to the process of planning and executing the conception, pricing, promotion, and distribution of ideas, goods, and services to create mutually beneficial exchanges.
Management	Management characterizes the process of leading and directing all or part of an organization, often a business, through the deployment and manipulation of resources. Early twentieth-century management writer Mary Parker Follett defined management as "the art of getting things done through people."
Marketing mix	The marketing mix approach to marketing is a model of crafting and implementing marketing strategies. It stresses the "mixing" or blending of various factors in such a way that both organizational and consumer (target markets) objectives are attained.
Budget	A financial plan that sets forth management's expectations for revenues and, based on those expectations, allocates the use of specific resources throughout the firm is called budget.

Go to **Cram101.com** for the Practice Tests for this Chapter.
And, **NEVER** highlight a book again!

Personal selling	Personal selling is interpersonal communication, often face to face, between a sales representative and an individual or group, usually with the objective of making a sale.
Publicity	Publicity refers to any information about an individual, product, or organization that's distributed to the public through the media and that's not paid for or controlled by the seller.
Corporation	A form of business organization that is owned by owners, called shareholders, who have no inherent right to manage the business, and is managed by a board of directors that is elected by the shareholders is called a corporation.
Sponsorship	When the advertiser assumes responsibility for the production and usually the content of a television program as well as the advertising that appears within it, we have sponsorship.
Contribution	In business organization law, the cash or property contributed to a business by its owners is referred to as contribution.
Remainder	A remainder in property law is a future interest created in a transferee that is capable of becoming possessory upon the natural termination of a prior estate created by the same instrument.
Target audience	That group that composes the present and potential prospects for a product or service is called the target audience.
Product Life Cycle	A theoretical model of what happens to sales and profits for a product over time is the product life cycle.
Communication objectives	Goals that an organization seeks to achieve through its promotional program in terms of communication effects such as creating awareness, knowledge, image, attitudes, preferences, or purchase intentions are communication objectives.
Brand awareness	How quickly or easily a given brand name comes to mind when a product category is mentioned is brand awareness.
Brand	A name, symbol, or design that identifies the goods or services of one seller or group of sellers and distinguishes them from the goods and services of competitors is a brand.
Trial	An examination before a competent tribunal, according to the law of the land, of the facts or law put in issue in a cause, for the purpose of determining such issue is a trial. When the court hears and determines any issue of fact or law for the purpose of determining the rights of the parties, it may be considered a trial.
Client	The organizations with the products, services, or causes to be marketed and for which advertising agencies and other marketing promotional firms provide services is referred to as a client.
Content	Content refers to all digital information included on a website, including the presentation form-text, video, audio, and graphics.
Consumer	A consumer is a individual or household that consume goods and services generated within the economy. Since this includes just about everyone, the term is a political term as much as an economic term when it is used in everyday speech.
Channel	Channel, in communications (sometimes called communications channel), refers to the medium used to convey information from a sender (or transmitter) to a receiver.
Communication channel	The pathways through which messages are communicated are called a communication channel.
Purchasing	Purchasing refers to the function in a firm that searches for quality material resources, finds the best suppliers, and negotiates the best price for goods and services.

Go to **Cram101.com** for the Practice Tests for this Chapter.
And, **NEVER** highlight a book again!

Coupon	In finance, a coupon is "attached" to bonds, either physically (as with old bonds) or electronically. Each coupon represents a predetermined payment promized to the bond-holder in return for his or her loan of money to the bond-issuer. The bond-holder is typically not the original lender, but receives this payment for effectively lending the money. The coupon rate (the amount promized per dollar of the face value of the bond) helps determine the interest rate or yield on the bond.
Distribution	Distribution is one of the four aspects of marketing. A distribution business is the middleman between the manufacturer and retailer or (usually)in commercial or industrial the business customer.
E-commerce	The sale of goods and services by computer over the Internet is referred to as the e-commerce.
Industry	Industry refers to a group of firms offering products that are close substitutes for each other.
Cognitive dissonance	The anxiety a person experiences when he or she simultaneously possesses two sets of knowledge or perceptions that are contradictory or incongruent is referred to as the cognitive dissonance.
Mass media	Mass media refers to non-personal channels of communication that allow a message to be sent to many individuals at one time.
Receiver	A person that is appointed as a custodian of other people's property by a court of law or a creditor of the owner, pending a lawsuit or reorganization is called a receiver.
Effective communication	When the intended meaning equals the perceived meaning it is called effective communication.
Insurance	A means for persons and businesses to protect themselves against the risk of loss is insurance.
Trust	Trust refers to a legal relationship in which a person who has legal title to property has the duty to hold it for the use or benefit of another person. The term is also used in a general sense to mean confidence reposed in one person by another.
Agent	One who acts under the direction of a principal for the principal's benefit in a legal relationship known as agency is called agent.
Customer contact	Customer contact refers to a characteristic of services that notes that customers tend to be more involved in the production of services than they are in manufactured goods.
Efficiency	Efficiency refers to the use of minimal resources, such as raw materials, money, and people-to produce a desired volume of output.
Consumer behavior	Consumer behavior refers to the actions a person takes in purchasing and using products and services, including the mental and social processes that precede and follow these actions.
Customer service	The ability of logistics management to satisfy users in terms of time, dependability, communication, and convenience is called the customer service.
E-business	E-business refers to work an organization does using electronic linkages; any business that takes place by digital processes over a computer network rather than in a physical space.
Expense	An expense refers to costs involved in operating a business, such as rent, utilities, and salaries.
Perceived risk	The anxieties felt because the consumer cannot anticipate the outcomes of a purchase but believes that there may be negative consequences is called a perceived risk.
Tangible	Having a physical existence is referred to as the tangible. Personal property other than real

Go to **Cram101.com** for the Practice Tests for this Chapter.
And, **NEVER** highlight a book again!

estate, such as cars, boats, stocks, or other assets.

Production	The creation of finished goods and services using the factors of production: land, labor, capital, entrepreneurship, and knowledge.
Contact personnel	The people at the 'front lines' who interact with the public in a service setting are contact personnel.
Personnel	A collective term for all of the employees of an organization. Personnel is also commonly used to refer to the personnel management function or the organizational unit responsible for administering personnel programs.
Layout	Layout refers to the physical arrangement of the various parts of an advertisement including the headline, subheads, illustrations, body copy, and any identifying marks.
Evaluation	The consumer's appraisal of the product or brand on important attributes is called evaluation.
Targeting	Targeting refers to the ability to address personalized promotions to a particular person who may be identified or described by means of an anonymous profile.
Advertisement	Advertisement is the promotion of goods, services, companies and ideas, usually by an identified sponsor. Marketers see advertising as part of an overall promotional strategy.
Advertising agency	A firm that specializes in the creation, production, and placement of advertising messages and may provide other services that facilitate the marketing communications process is an advertising agency.
Agency	Agency refers to a legal relationship in which an agent acts under the direction of a principal for the principal's benefit. Also used to refer to government regulatory bodies of all kinds.
Tactic	A short-term immediate decision that, in its totality, leads to the achievement of strategic goals is called a tactic.
Contract	A contract is a "promise" or an "agreement" that is enforced or recognized by the law. In the civil law, contracts are considered to be part of the general law of obligations. This article describes the law relating to contracts in common law jurisdictions.
Competition	In business, competition occurs when rival organizations with similar products and services attempt to gain customers.
Discount	A discount is the reduction of the base price of a product.
Advertising campaign	A comprehensive advertising plan that consists of a series of messages in a variety of media that center on a single theme or idea is referred to as an advertising campaign.
Level of service	The degree of service provided to the customer by self, limited, and full-service retailers is referred to as the level of service.
Bottom line	Bottom line refers to the last line in a profit and loss statement; it refers to net profit.
Consideration	Consideration in contract law, a basic requirement for an enforceable agreement under traditional contract principles, defined in this text as legal value, bargained for and given in exchange for an act or promise. In corporation law, cash or property contributed to a corporation in exchange for shares, or a promise to contribute such cash or property.
Intangibility	A unique element of services-services cannot be held, touched, or seen before the purchase decision which is referred to as intangibility.
Inseparability	Inseparability is a characteristic of services, which describes how service products tend to be produced at the same time as they are consumed.

Go to **Cram101.com** for the Practice Tests for this Chapter.

Go to **Cram101.com** for the Practice Tests for this Chapter.
And, **NEVER** highlight a book again!

Principal	In agency law, one under whose direction an agent acts and for whose benefit that agent acts is a principal.
Empathy	Empathy refers to dimension of service quality-caring individualized attention provided to customers.
Tangibles	Dimension of service quality-appearance of physical facilities, equipment, personnel, and communication materials are called tangibles.
Tax accountant	An accountant trained in tax law and responsible for preparing tax returns or developing tax strategies is called a tax accountant.
Accountability	The extent to which one must answer to higher authority-legal or organizational-for one's actions in society at large or within one's particular organizational position is an accountability.
Credibility	The extent to which a source is perceived as having knowledge, skill, or experience relevant to a communication topic and can be trusted to give an unbiased opinion or present objective information on the issue is called credibility.
Quality control	The measurement of products and services against set standards is referred to as quality control.
Cash flow	In finance, cash flow refers to the amounts of cash being received and spent by a business during a defined period of time, sometimes tied to a specific project. Most of the time they are being used to determine gaps in the liquid position of a company.
Closing	The finalization of a real estate sales transaction that passes title to the property from the seller to the buyer is referred to as a closing. Closing is a sales term which refers to the process of making a sale. It refers to reaching the final step, which may be an exchange of money or acquiring a signature.
Marketing communication	The communication components of marketing, which include public relations, advertising, personal selling, and sales promotion is a marketing communication.
Jury	A body of lay persons, selected by lot, or by some other fair and impartial means, to ascertain, under the guidance of the judge, the truth in questions of fact arising either in civil litigation or a criminal process is referred to as jury.
Knowledge base	Knowledge base refers to a database that includes decision rules for use of the data, which may be qualitative as well as quantitative.
Positioning strategies	The strategies used in positioning a brand or product are positioning strategies.
Marketing strategy	Marketing strategy refers to the means by which a marketing goal is to be achieved, usually characterized by a specified target market and a marketing program to reach it.
Revenue	Revenue refers to the total amount of money a business earns in a given period by selling goods and services. The value of what is received for goods sold, services rendered.
Halo effect	Halo effect refers to a more specific perceptual bias that affects perceptions of others; in particular, the use of one piece of information observed about a person to infer other characteristics that may or may not true.
Logo	Logo refers to device or other brand name that cannot be spoken.
Stock	In financial terminology, stock is the capital raized by a corporation, through the issuance and sale of shares. A shareholder is any person or organization which owns one or more shares of a corporation's stock. The aggregate value of a corporation's issued shares is its market capitalization.

Go to **Cram101.com** for the Practice Tests for this Chapter.

Go to **Cram101.com** for the Practice Tests for this Chapter.
And, **NEVER** highlight a book again!

Holding	The holding is a court's determination of a matter of law based on the issue presented in the particular case. In other words: under this law, with these facts, this result.
Sales promotion	Sales promotion refers to the promotional tool that stimulates consumer purchasing and dealer interest by means of short-term activities.
Decline stage	The fourth and last stage of the product life cycle when sales and profits begin to drop is called the decline stage.
Options	Options give the owner the right but not the obligation to buy or sell an underlying security at a set price for a given time period.
Accounting	The recording, classifying, summarizing, and interpreting of financial events and transactions to provide management and other interested parties the information they need to make good decisions is called accounting.

78

Go to **Cram101.com** for the Practice Tests for this Chapter.

Go to **Cram101.com** for the Practice Tests for this Chapter.
And, **NEVER** highlight a book again!

Customer service	The ability of logistics management to satisfy users in terms of time, dependability, communication, and convenience is called the customer service.
Marketing	The American Marketing Association suggests that Marketing is "the process of planning and executing the pricing, promotion, and distribution of goods, ideas, and services to create exchanges that satisfy individual and organizational goals."
Tangible	Having a physical existence is referred to as the tangible. Personal property other than real estate, such as cars, boats, stocks, or other assets.
Personnel	A collective term for all of the employees of an organization. Personnel is also commonly used to refer to the personnel management function or the organizational unit responsible for administering personnel programs.
Evaluation	The consumer's appraisal of the product or brand on important attributes is called evaluation.
Intangibility	A unique element of services-services cannot be held, touched, or seen before the purchase decision which is referred to as intangibility.
Layout	Layout refers to the physical arrangement of the various parts of an advertisement including the headline, subheads, illustrations, body copy, and any identifying marks.
Tangibles	Dimension of service quality-appearance of physical facilities, equipment, personnel, and communication materials are called tangibles.
Customer retention	Customer retention refers to the percentage of customers who return to a service provider or continue to purchase a manufactured product.
Insurance	A means for persons and businesses to protect themselves against the risk of loss is insurance.
Management	Management characterizes the process of leading and directing all or part of an organization, often a business, through the deployment and manipulation of resources. Early twentieth-century management writer Mary Parker Follett defined management as "the art of getting things done through people."
Perceived risk	The anxieties felt because the consumer cannot anticipate the outcomes of a purchase but believes that there may be negative consequences is called a perceived risk.
Cognitive dissonance	The anxiety a person experiences when he or she simultaneously possesses two sets of knowledge or perceptions that are contradictory or incongruent is referred to as the cognitive dissonance.
Production	The creation of finished goods and services using the factors of production: land, labor, capital, entrepreneurship, and knowledge.
Core	A core is the set of feasible allocations in an economy that cannot be improved upon by subset of the set of the economy's consumers (a coalition).
Organizational goals	Objectives that management seeks to achieve in pursuing the firm's purpose are organizational goals.
Controlling	A management function that involves determining whether or not an organization is progressing toward its goals and objectives, and taking corrective action if it is not is called controlling.
Market segments	Market segments refer to the groups that result from the process of market segmentation; these groups ideally have common needs and will respond similarly to a marketing action.
Competitor	Other organizations in the same industry or type of business that provide a good or service to the same set of customers is referred to as a competitor.

Go to **Cram101.com** for the Practice Tests for this Chapter.
And, **NEVER** highlight a book again!

Economy	The income, expenditures, and resources that affect the cost of running a business and household are called an economy.
Discount	A discount is the reduction of the base price of a product.
Budget	A financial plan that sets forth management's expectations for revenues and, based on those expectations, allocates the use of specific resources throughout the firm is called budget.
Industry	Industry refers to a group of firms offering products that are close substitutes for each other.
Product	Any physical good, service, or idea that satisfies a want or need is called product. Product in project management is a physical entity created as a result of project work.
Brand	A name, symbol, or design that identifies the goods or services of one seller or group of sellers and distinguishes them from the goods and services of competitors is a brand.
Users	Users refer to people in the organization who actually use the product or service purchased by the buying center.
Advertising	Advertising refers to paid, nonpersonal communication through various media by organizations and individuals who are in some way identified in the advertising message.
Bottom line	Bottom line refers to the last line in a profit and loss statement; it refers to net profit.
Consumer behavior	Consumer behavior refers to the actions a person takes in purchasing and using products and services, including the mental and social processes that precede and follow these actions.
Consumer	A consumer is a individual or household that consume goods and services generated within the economy. Since this includes just about everyone, the term is a political term as much as an economic term when it is used in everyday speech.
Context	The effect of the background under which a message often takes on more and richer meaning is a context. Context is especially important in cross-cultural interactions because some cultures are said to be high context or low context.
Retailing	All activities involved in selling, renting, and providing goods and services to ultimate consumers for personal, family, or household use is referred to as retailing.
Appeal	Appeal refers to the act of asking an appellate court to overturn a decision after the trial court's final judgment has been entered.
Exhibit	Exhibit refers to a copy of a written instrument on which a pleading is founded, annexed to the pleading and by reference made a part of it. Any paper or thing offered in evidence and marked for identification.
Comprehensive	A comprehensive refers to a layout accurate in size, color, scheme, and other necessary details to show how a final ad will look. For presentation only, never for reproduction.
Utility	An economic term that refers to the value or want-satisfying ability that's added to goods or services by organizations when the products are made more useful or accessible to consumers than before is a utility.
Productivity	Productivity refers to the total output of goods and services in a given period of time divided by work hours.
Target market	One or more specific groups of potential consumers toward which an organization directs its marketing program are a target market.
Fixture	Fixture refers to a thing that was originally personal property and that has been actually or constructively affixed to the soil itself or to some structure legally a part of the land.
Nonverbal	The many additional ways that communication is accomplished beyond the oral or written word

Go to **Cram101.com** for the Practice Tests for this Chapter.

Go to **Cram101.com** for the Practice Tests for this Chapter.
And, **NEVER** highlight a book again!

communication	is referred to as nonverbal communication.
Communication	Communication refers to the social process in which two or more parties exchange information and share meaning.
Assessment	Collecting information and providing feedback to employees about their behavior, communication style, or skills is an assessment.
Assignment	A transfer of property or some right or interest is referred to as assignment.
Positioning	The art and science of fitting the product or service to one or more segments of the market in such a way as to set it meaningfully apart from competition is called positioning.
Forming	The first stage of team development, where the team is formed and the objectives for the team are set is referred to as forming.
Inseparability	Inseparability is a characteristic of services, which describes how service products tend to be produced at the same time as they are consumed.
Configuration	An organization's shape, which reflects the division of labor and the means of coordinating the divided tasks is configuration.
Tactic	A short-term immediate decision that, in its totality, leads to the achievement of strategic goals is called a tactic.
Buyer	A buyer refers to a role in the buying center with formal authority and responsibility to select the supplier and negotiate the terms of the contract.
Visibility	Visibility is used in marketing, as a measure of how much the public sees a product or its advertising.
Consideration	Consideration in contract law, a basic requirement for an enforceable agreement under traditional contract principles, defined in this text as legal value, bargained for and given in exchange for an act or promise. In corporation law, cash or property contributed to a corporation in exchange for shares, or a promise to contribute such cash or property.
Compatibility	Compatibility refers to used to describe a product characteristic, it means a good fit with other products used by the consumer or with the consumer's lifestyle. Used in a technical context, it means the ability of systems to work together.
Options	Options give the owner the right but not the obligation to buy or sell an underlying security at a set price for a given time period.
Efficiency	Efficiency refers to the use of minimal resources, such as raw materials, money, and people- to produce a desired volume of output.
Gross margin	How much a firm earned by buying and selling merchandise is a gross margin. It is an ambiguous phrase that expresses the relationship between gross profit and sales revenue.
Margin	A deposit by a buyer in stocks with a seller or a stockbroker, as security to cover fluctuations in the market in reference to stocks that the buyer has purchased but for which he has not paid is a margin. Commodities are also traded on margin.
Manager	A person who is formally responsible for supporting the work efforts of other people is a manager.
Customer contact	Customer contact refers to a characteristic of services that notes that customers tend to be more involved in the production of services than they are in manufactured goods.

Go to **Cram101.com** for the Practice Tests for this Chapter.
And, **NEVER** highlight a book again!

Manager	A person who is formally responsible for supporting the work efforts of other people is a manager.
Contact personnel	The people at the 'front lines' who interact with the public in a service setting are contact personnel.
Personnel	A collective term for all of the employees of an organization. Personnel is also commonly used to refer to the personnel management function or the organizational unit responsible for administering personnel programs.
Boundary-spanning roles	Roles assumed by people and/or departments that link and coordinate the organization with key elements in the external environment are referred to as boundary-spanning roles.
Marketing	The American Marketing Association suggests that Marketing is "the process of planning and executing the pricing, promotion, and distribution of goods, ideas, and services to create exchanges that satisfy individual and organizational goals."
Empowerment	Giving employees the authority and responsibility to respond quickly to customer requests is called empowerment.
Contingency approach	Contingency approach refers to the dominant perspective in organizational behavior, it argues that there's no single best way to manage behavior. What 'works' in any given context depends on the complex interplay between a variety of person and situational factors.
Complexity	The technical sophistication of the product and hence the amount of understanding required to use it is referred to as complexity. It is the opposite of simplicity.
Industry	Industry refers to a group of firms offering products that are close substitutes for each other.
Interest	Interest refers to the payment the issuer of the bond makes to the bondholders for use of the borrowed money. It is the return to capital achieved over time or as the result of an event.
E-commerce	The sale of goods and services by computer over the Internet is referred to as the e-commerce.
Brand	A name, symbol, or design that identifies the goods or services of one seller or group of sellers and distinguishes them from the goods and services of competitors is a brand.
Budget	A financial plan that sets forth management's expectations for revenues and, based on those expectations, allocates the use of specific resources throughout the firm is called budget.
Product differentiation	The creation of real or perceived product differences is called product differentiation.
Product	Any physical good, service, or idea that satisfies a want or need is called product. Product in project management is a physical entity created as a result of project work.
Competitive advantage	A business is said to have a competitive advantage when its unique strengths, often based on cost, quality, time, and innovation, offer consumers a greater percieved value and there by diffretiating it from its competitors.
Staffing	Staffing refers to a management function that includes hiring, motivating, and retaining the best people available to accomplish the company's objectives.
Competitor	Other organizations in the same industry or type of business that provide a good or service to the same set of customers is referred to as a competitor.
Client	The organizations with the products, services, or causes to be marketed and for which advertising agencies and other marketing promotional firms provide services is referred to as a client.

Go to Cram101.com for the Practice Tests for this Chapter.

Go to **Cram101.com** for the Practice Tests for this Chapter.
And, **NEVER** highlight a book again!

Organizational Behavior	The study of human behavior in organizational settings, the interface between human behavior and the organization, and the organization itself is called organizational behavior.
Compromise	Compromise occurs when the interaction is moderately important to meeting goals and the goals are neither completely compatible nor completely incompatible.
Regulation	Regulation refers to restrictions state and federal laws place on business with regard to the conduct of its activities.
Franchise	A business established or operated under an authorization to sell or distribute a company's goods or services in a particular area is a franchise.
Public relations	Public relations refers to the management function that evaluates public attitudes, changes policies and procedures in response to the public's requests, and executes a program of action and information to earn public understanding and acceptance.
Advertising	Advertising refers to paid, nonpersonal communication through various media by organizations and individuals who are in some way identified in the advertising message.
Advertisement	Advertisement is the promotion of goods, services, companies and ideas, usually by an identified sponsor. Marketers see advertising as part of an overall promotional strategy.
Inseparability	Inseparability is a characteristic of services, which describes how service products tend to be produced at the same time as they are consumed.
Management	Management characterizes the process of leading and directing all or part of an organization, often a business, through the deployment and manipulation of resources. Early twentieth-century management writer Mary Parker Follett defined management as "the art of getting things done through people."
Human resources	Human resources refers to the individuals within the firm, and to the portion of the firm's organization that deals with hiring, firing, training, and other personnel issues.
Hierarchy	A system of grouping people in an organization according to rank from the top down in which all subordinate managers must report to one person is called a hierarchy.
Open system	A system that interacts with its environment is referred to as open system. It is a system that takes in (raw materials, capital, skilled labor) and converts them into goods and services (via machinery, human skills) that are sent back to that environment, where they are bought by customers.
Automation	Automation allows machines to do work previously accomplished by people.
Estate	An estate is the totality of the legal rights, interests, entitlements and obligations attaching to property. In the context of wills and probate, it refers to the totality of the property which the deceased owned or in which some interest was held.
Mortgage	A conveyance of property to secure the performance of some obligation, the conveyance to be void on the due performance thereof is referred to as the mortgage.
Performance feedback	The process of providing employees with information regarding their performance effectiveness is referred to as performance feedback.
Equity	Equity is the name given to the set of legal principles, in countries following the English common law tradition, which supplement strict rules of law where their application would operate harshly, so as to achieve what is sometimes referred to as "natural justice."
Compensation	A payment that is given or recieved as reparation for a service or loss is referred to as compensation.
Customer contact	Customer contact refers to a characteristic of services that notes that customers tend to be more involved in the production of services than they are in manufactured goods.

Go to **Cram101.com** for the Practice Tests for this Chapter.
And, **NEVER** highlight a book again!

Health insurance	Health insurance is a type of insurance whereby the insurer pays the medical costs of the insured if the insured becomes sick due to covered causes, or due to accidents. The insurer may be a private organization or a government agency.
Insurance	A means for persons and businesses to protect themselves against the risk of loss is insurance.
Retailing	All activities involved in selling, renting, and providing goods and services to ultimate consumers for personal, family, or household use is referred to as retailing.
Malcolm Baldrige National Quality Award	Malcolm Baldrige national quality award refers to U.S. national quality award sponsored by the U.S. Department of Commerce and private industry. The program aims to reward quality in the business sector, health care, and education, and was inspired by the ideas of Total Quality Management.
Contract	A contract is a "promise" or an "agreement" that is enforced or recognized by the law. In the civil law, contracts are considered to be part of the general law of obligations. This article describes the law relating to contracts in common law jurisdictions.
Recruitment	Recruitment refers to the set of activities used to obtain a sufficient number of the right people at the right time; its purpose is to select those who best meet the needs of the organization.
Quality circle	A quality circle is a volunteer group composed of workers who meet together to discuss workplace improvement, and make presentations to management with their ideas.
Brainstorming	Brainstorming refers to a technique designed to overcome our natural tendency to evaluate and criticize ideas and thereby reduce the creative output of those ideas. People are encouraged to produce ideas/options without criticizing, often at a very fast pace to minimize our natural tendency to criticize.
Content	Content refers to all digital information included on a website, including the presentation form-text, video, audio, and graphics.
Teamwork	That which occurs when group members work together in ways that utilize their skills well to accomplish a purpose is called teamwork.
Profit sharing	A compenzation plan in which payments are based on a measure of organization performance and do not become part of the employees' base salary is profit sharing.
Agent	One who acts under the direction of a principal for the principal's benefit in a legal relationship known as agency is called agent.
Broker	An agent who bargains or carries on negotiations in behalf of the principal as an intermediary between the latter and third persons in transacting business relative to the acquisition of contractual rights, or to the sale or purchase of property the custody of which is not entrusted to him or her for the purpose of discharging the agency is called a broker.
Theory Y	Theory Y refers to concept described by Douglas McGregor reflecting an approach to management that takes a positive and optimistic perspective on workers.
Financial manager	Managers who make recommendations to top executives regarding strategies for improving the financial strength of a firm are referred to as a financial manager.
Theory X	Theory X refers to concept described by Douglas McGregor indicating an approach to management that takes a negative and pessimistic view of workers.
Interpersonal skills	Interpersonal skills are used to communicate with, understand, and motivate individuals and groups.

Go to **Cram101.com** for the Practice Tests for this Chapter.

Go to **Cram101.com** for the Practice Tests for this Chapter.
And, **NEVER** highlight a book again!

Competition	In business, competition occurs when rival organizations with similar products and services attempt to gain customers.
Productivity	Productivity refers to the total output of goods and services in a given period of time divided by work hours.
Production	The creation of finished goods and services using the factors of production: land, labor, capital, entrepreneurship, and knowledge.
Loyalty	Marketers tend to define customer loyalty as making repeat purchases. Some argue that it should be defined attitudinally as a strongly positive feeling about the brand.
Copyright	Copyright refers to a set of exclusive rights, protected by federal law, pertaining to certain creative works such as books, musical compositions, computer programs, works of art, and so forth. The rights are to reproduce the work in question, to prepare derivative works based on it, to sell or otherwise distribute it, and to perform or display it publicly.
Customer retention	Customer retention refers to the percentage of customers who return to a service provider or continue to purchase a manufactured product.
Revenue	Revenue refers to the total amount of money a business earns in a given period by selling goods and services. The value of what is received for goods sold, services rendered.
Intangibility	A unique element of services-services cannot be held, touched, or seen before the purchase decision which is referred to as intangibility.
Attachment	Attachment in general, the process of taking a person's property under an appropriate judicial order by an appropriate officer of the court. Used for a variety of purposes, including the acquisition of jurisdiction over the property seized and the securing of property that may be used to satisfy a debt.
Human resource planning	Forecasting the organization's human resource needs, developing replacement charts for all levels of the organization, and preparing inventories of the skills and abilities individuals need to move within the organization is called human resource planning.
Marketing management	Marketing management refers to the process of planning and executing the conception, pricing, promotion, and distribution of ideas, goods, and services to create mutually beneficial exchanges.
Human resource management	The process of evaluating human resource needs, finding people to fill those needs, and getting the best work from each employee by providing the right incentives and job environment, all with the goal of meeting the needs of the firm are called human resource management.
Resource management	Resource management is the efficient and effective deployment of an organization's resources when they are needed. Such resources may include financial resources, inventory, human skills, production resources, or information technology.

Go to **Cram101.com** for the Practice Tests for this Chapter.

Go to **Cram101.com** for the Practice Tests for this Chapter.
And, **NEVER** highlight a book again!

Production	The creation of finished goods and services using the factors of production: land, labor, capital, entrepreneurship, and knowledge.
Exchange	The trade of things of value between buyer and seller so that each is better off after the trade is called the exchange.
Participation	Participation refers to the process of giving employees a voice in making decisions about their own work.
Customer relationship management	Learning as much as possible about customers and doing everything you can to satisfy them or even delight them with goods and services over time is customer relationship management.
Relationship management	A method for developing long-term associations with customers is referred to as relationship management.
Management	Management characterizes the process of leading and directing all or part of an organization, often a business, through the deployment and manipulation of resources. Early twentieth-century management writer Mary Parker Follett defined management as "the art of getting things done through people."
Bureaucracy	Bureaucracy refers to an organization with many layers of managers who set rules and regulations and oversee all decisions.
Customer retention	Customer retention refers to the percentage of customers who return to a service provider or continue to purchase a manufactured product.
Customer contact	Customer contact refers to a characteristic of services that notes that customers tend to be more involved in the production of services than they are in manufactured goods.
Efficiency	Efficiency refers to the use of minimal resources, such as raw materials, money, and people- to produce a desired volume of output.
Market segments	Market segments refer to the groups that result from the process of market segmentation; these groups ideally have common needs and will respond similarly to a marketing action.
Human resources	Human resources refers to the individuals within the firm, and to the portion of the firm's organization that deals with hiring, firing, training, and other personnel issues.
Marketing	The American Marketing Association suggests that Marketing is "the process of planning and executing the pricing, promotion, and distribution of goods, ideas, and services to create exchanges that satisfy individual and organizational goals."
Job analysis	Job analysis refers to a study of what is done by employees who hold various job titles. It refers to various methodologies for analyzing the requirements of a job.
Standing	Standing refers to the legal requirement that anyone seeking to challenge a particular action in court must demonstrate that such action substantially affects his legitimate interests before he will be entitled to bring suit.
Personnel	A collective term for all of the employees of an organization. Personnel is also commonly used to refer to the personnel management function or the organizational unit responsible for administering personnel programs.
Staffing	Staffing refers to a management function that includes hiring, motivating, and retaining the best people available to accomplish the company's objectives.
Options	Options give the owner the right but not the obligation to buy or sell an underlying security at a set price for a given time period.
Competitor	Other organizations in the same industry or type of business that provide a good or service to the same set of customers is referred to as a competitor.

Go to **Cram101.com** for the Practice Tests for this Chapter.
And, **NEVER** highlight a book again!

Incentive	A reward offered by a marketer to a prospective customer in return for furnishing information or making a purchase is referred to as an incentive.
Trial	An examination before a competent tribunal, according to the law of the land, of the facts or law put in issue in a cause, for the purpose of determining such issue is a trial. When the court hears and determines any issue of fact or law for the purpose of determining the rights of the parties, it may be considered a trial.
Promotion	Promotion refers to all the techniques sellers use to motivate people to buy products or services. An attempt by marketers to inform people about products and to persuade them to participate in an exchange.
Mistake	In contract law a mistake is incorrect understanding by one or more parties to a contract and may be used as grounds to invalidate the agreement. Common law has identified three different types of mistake in contract: unilateral mistake, mutual mistake, and common mistake.
Personalization	The consumer-initiated practice of generating content on a marketer's website that is custom tailored to an individual's specific needs and preferences is called personalization.
Trust	Trust refers to a legal relationship in which a person who has legal title to property has the duty to hold it for the use or benefit of another person. The term is also used in a general sense to mean confidence reposed in one person by another.
Consumer behavior	Consumer behavior refers to the actions a person takes in purchasing and using products and services, including the mental and social processes that precede and follow these actions.
Consumer	A consumer is a individual or household that consume goods and services generated within the economy. Since this includes just about everyone, the term is a political term as much as an economic term when it is used in everyday speech.
Preparation	Preparation refers to usually the first stage in the creative process. It includes education and formal training.
Manager	A person who is formally responsible for supporting the work efforts of other people is a manager.
Tactic	A short-term immediate decision that, in its totality, leads to the achievement of strategic goals is called a tactic.
Inseparability	Inseparability is a characteristic of services, which describes how service products tend to be produced at the same time as they are consumed.
Industry	Industry refers to a group of firms offering products that are close substitutes for each other.
Grant	Grant refers to an intergovernmental transfer of funds . Since the New Deal, state and local governments have become increasingly dependent upon federal grants for an almost infinite variety of programs.
Chancellor	A handful of U.S. states, like Delaware, still maintain a separate Court of Chancery with jurisdiction over equity cases. Judges who sit on those courts is called a chancellor.
Bond	A long-term debt security that is secured by collateral is called a bond.
Categorizing	The act of placing strengths and weaknesses into categories in generic internal assessment is called categorizing.
Contact personnel	The people at the 'front lines' who interact with the public in a service setting are contact personnel.
Customer service	The ability of logistics management to satisfy users in terms of time, dependability, communication, and convenience is called the customer service.

Go to **Cram101.com** for the Practice Tests for this Chapter.

Go to **Cram101.com** for the Practice Tests for this Chapter.
And, **NEVER** highlight a book again!

Consideration	Consideration in contract law, a basic requirement for an enforceable agreement under traditional contract principles, defined in this text as legal value, bargained for and given in exchange for an act or promise. In corporation law, cash or property contributed to a corporation in exchange for shares, or a promise to contribute such cash or property.
Policy	Similar to a script in that a policy can be a less than completely rational decision-making method. Involves the use of a pre-existing set of decision steps for any problem that presents itself.
Appeal	Appeal refers to the act of asking an appellate court to overturn a decision after the trial court's final judgment has been entered.
Remainder	A remainder in property law is a future interest created in a transferee that is capable of becoming possessory upon the natural termination of a prior estate created by the same instrument.
Credibility	The extent to which a source is perceived as having knowledge, skill, or experience relevant to a communication topic and can be trusted to give an unbiased opinion or present objective information on the issue is called credibility.
Better Business Bureau	An organization established and funded by businesses that operates primarily at the local level to monitor activities of companies and promote fair advertising and selling practices is a better business bureau.
Closing	The finalization of a real estate sales transaction that passes title to the property from the seller to the buyer is referred to as a closing. Closing is a sales term which refers to the process of making a sale. It refers to reaching the final step, which may be an exchange of money or acquiring a signature.
Deed	A deed is a legal instrument used to grant a right. The deed is best known as the method of transferring title to real estate from one person to another.
Targeting	Targeting refers to the ability to address personalized promotions to a particular person who may be identified or described by means of an anonymous profile.
Client	The organizations with the products, services, or causes to be marketed and for which advertising agencies and other marketing promotional firms provide services is referred to as a client.
Revenue	Revenue refers to the total amount of money a business earns in a given period by selling goods and services. The value of what is received for goods sold, services rendered.
Brand	A name, symbol, or design that identifies the goods or services of one seller or group of sellers and distinguishes them from the goods and services of competitors is a brand.
General manager	A manager who is responsible for several departments that perform different functions is called general manager.
Utility	An economic term that refers to the value or want-satisfying ability that's added to goods or services by organizations when the products are made more useful or accessible to consumers than before is a utility.
Asset	In business and accounting an asset is anything owned which can produce future economic benefit, whether in possession or by right to take possession, by a person or a group acting together, e.g. a company, the measurement of which can be expressed in monetary terms. Asset is listed on the balance sheet. It has a normal balance of debit.
Agent	One who acts under the direction of a principal for the principal's benefit in a legal relationship known as agency is called agent.
Argument	The discussion by counsel for the respective parties of their contentions on the law and the

Go to **Cram101.com** for the Practice Tests for this Chapter.

Go to **Cram101.com** for the Practice Tests for this Chapter.
And, **NEVER** highlight a book again!

	facts of the case being tried in order to aid the jury in arriving at a correct and just conclusion is called argument.
Coupon	In finance, a coupon is "attached" to bonds, either physically (as with old bonds) or electronically. Each coupon represents a predetermined payment promized to the bond-holder in return for his or her loan of money to the bond-issuer. The bond-holder is typically not the original lender, but receives this payment for effectively lending the money. The coupon rate (the amount promized per dollar of the face value of the bond) helps determine the interest rate or yield on the bond.
Council of better business	Council of better business refers to the development of codes and standards for ethical and responsible business and advertising practices.
Hearing	A hearing is a proceeding before a court or other decision-making body or officer. A hearing is generally distinguished from a trial in that it is usually shorter and often less formal.
Capital	Contributions of money and other property to a business made by the owners of the business are capital.
Social security	The term used to describe the Old-Age, Survivors, and Disability Insurance Program established by the Social Security Act of 1935 is social security.
Customer relationship management systems	Systems that help companies track customers' interaction with the firm and allow employees to call up information on past transactions are referred to as customer relationship management systems.
Management system	A management system is the framework of processes and procedures used to ensure that an organization can fulfill all tasks required to achieve its objectives.
Productivity	Productivity refers to the total output of goods and services in a given period of time divided by work hours.

Go to **Cram101.com** for the Practice Tests for this Chapter.

Go to **Cram101.com** for the Practice Tests for this Chapter.
And, **NEVER** highlight a book again!

Customer retention	Customer retention refers to the percentage of customers who return to a service provider or continue to purchase a manufactured product.
Manager	A person who is formally responsible for supporting the work efforts of other people is a manager.
Marketing	The American Marketing Association suggests that Marketing is "the process of planning and executing the pricing, promotion, and distribution of goods, ideas, and services to create exchanges that satisfy individual and organizational goals."
Advertising	Advertising refers to paid, nonpersonal communication through various media by organizations and individuals who are in some way identified in the advertising message.
Mission statement	Mission statement refers to an outline of the fundamental purposes of an organization.
Consumerism	Consumerism refers to a social movement that seeks to increase and strengthen the rights and powers of buyers in relation to sellers.
Customer service	The ability of logistics management to satisfy users in terms of time, dependability, communication, and convenience is called the customer service.
Inflation	A general rise in the prices of goods and services over time is an inflation. It is a change in some important measure of money which says either real or apparent value is falling.
Deregulation	Deregulation refers to government withdrawal of certain laws and regulations that seem to hinder competition.
Competition	In business, competition occurs when rival organizations with similar products and services attempt to gain customers.
Expense	An expense refers to costs involved in operating a business, such as rent, utilities, and salaries.
Automation	Automation allows machines to do work previously accomplished by people.
Efficiency	Efficiency refers to the use of minimal resources, such as raw materials, money, and people-to produce a desired volume of output.
Quality control	The measurement of products and services against set standards is referred to as quality control.
Market share	The ratio of sales revenue of the firm to the total sales revenue of all firms in the industry, including the firm itself is the market share.
Gross domestic product	The total value of goods and services produced in a country in a given year is a gross domestic product. It is one of several measures of the size of its economy.
Product	Any physical good, service, or idea that satisfies a want or need is called product. Product in project management is a physical entity created as a result of project work.
Mistake	In contract law a mistake is incorrect understanding by one or more parties to a contract and may be used as grounds to invalidate the agreement. Common law has identified three different types of mistake in contract: unilateral mistake, mutual mistake, and common mistake.
Bottom line	Bottom line refers to the last line in a profit and loss statement; it refers to net profit.
Industry	Industry refers to a group of firms offering products that are close substitutes for each other.
Net present value	Net present value refers to the present value of the cash inflows minus the present value of the cash outflows with the cost of capital used as a discount rate. This method is used to evaluate capital budgeting projects.

Go to **Cram101.com** for the Practice Tests for this Chapter.
And, **NEVER** highlight a book again!

Present value	Present value refers to the current or discounted value of a future sum or annuity. The value is discounted back at a given interest rate for a specified time period.
Complaint	The pleading in a civil case in which the plaintiff states his claim and requests relief is called complaint. In the common law, it is a formal legal document that sets out the basic facts and legal reasons that the filing party (the plaintiffs) believes are sufficient to support a claim against another person, persons, entity or entities (the defendants) that entitles the plaintiff(s) to a remedy (either money damages or injunctive relief).
Competitor	Other organizations in the same industry or type of business that provide a good or service to the same set of customers is referred to as a competitor.
Communication	Communication refers to the social process in which two or more parties exchange information and share meaning.
Loyalty	Marketers tend to define customer loyalty as making repeat purchases. Some argue that it should be defined attitudinally as a strongly positive feeling about the brand.
Confirmed	When the seller's bank agrees to assume liability on the letter of credit issued by the buyer's bank the transaction is confirmed. The term means that the credit is not only backed up by the issuing foreign bank, but that payment is also guaranteed by the notifying American bank.
Customer defection	Customer defection refers to customers who do not continue to purchase from the enterprise. The words attrition and churn are often used to describe the same phenomenon.
Publicity	Publicity refers to any information about an individual, product, or organization that's distributed to the public through the media and that's not paid for or controlled by the seller.
Respondent	Respondent refers to a term often used to describe the party charged in an administrative proceeding. The party adverse to the appellant in a case appealed to a higher court.
Agent	One who acts under the direction of a principal for the principal's benefit in a legal relationship known as agency is called agent.
Compensation	A payment that is given or recieved as reparation for a service or loss is referred to as compensation.
Sales management	Planning the selling program and implementing and controlling the personal selling effort of the firm is called sales management.
Management	Management characterizes the process of leading and directing all or part of an organization, often a business, through the deployment and manipulation of resources. Early twentieth-century management writer Mary Parker Follett defined management as "the art of getting things done through people."
Corporate advertising	Advertising designed to promote overall awareness of a company or enhance its image among a target audience is referred to as corporate advertising.
Hierarchy	A system of grouping people in an organization according to rank from the top down in which all subordinate managers must report to one person is called a hierarchy.
Continuous improvement	Constantly improving the way the organization does things so that customer needs can be better satisfied is referred to as continuous improvement.
Distribution	Distribution is one of the four aspects of marketing. A distribution business is the middleman between the manufacturer and retailer or (usually)in commercial or industrial the business customer.
Discount	A discount is the reduction of the base price of a product.

104

Go to **Cram101.com** for the Practice Tests for this Chapter.

Go to **Cram101.com** for the Practice Tests for this Chapter.
And, **NEVER** highlight a book again!

Argument	The discussion by counsel for the respective parties of their contentions on the law and the facts of the case being tried in order to aid the jury in arriving at a correct and just conclusion is called argument.
Context	The effect of the background under which a message often takes on more and richer meaning is a context. Context is especially important in cross-cultural interactions because some cultures are said to be high context or low context.
Cognitive dissonance	The anxiety a person experiences when he or she simultaneously possesses two sets of knowledge or perceptions that are contradictory or incongruent is referred to as the cognitive dissonance.
Consideration	Consideration in contract law, a basic requirement for an enforceable agreement under traditional contract principles, defined in this text as legal value, bargained for and given in exchange for an act or promise. In corporation law, cash or property contributed to a corporation in exchange for shares, or a promise to contribute such cash or property.
Personnel	A collective term for all of the employees of an organization. Personnel is also commonly used to refer to the personnel management function or the organizational unit responsible for administering personnel programs.
Hawthorne effect	The tendency for people to behave differently when they know they are being studied is called the Hawthorne Effect.
Benchmarking	Discovering how others do something better than your own firm so you can imitate or leapfrog competition is called benchmarking.
Beneficiary	The person for whose benefit an insurance policy, trust, will, or contract is established is a beneficiary. In the case of a contract, the beneficiary is called a third-party beneficiary.
Credibility	The extent to which a source is perceived as having knowledge, skill, or experience relevant to a communication topic and can be trusted to give an unbiased opinion or present objective information on the issue is called credibility.
Internal customer	An individuals or unit within the firm that receives services from other entities within the organization is an internal customer.
Innovation	The process of creating and doing new things that are introduced into the marketplace as products, processes, or services is innovation.
Demographics	Demographics is a shorthand term for 'population characteristics'. Demographics include race, age, income, mobility (in terms of travel time to work or number of vehicles available), educational attainment, home ownership, employment status, and even location. Demographics are primarily used in economic and marketing research.
Demographic	A demographic is a term used in marketing and broadcasting, to describe a demographic grouping or a market segment.
Level of service	The degree of service provided to the customer by self, limited, and full-service retailers is referred to as the level of service.
Evaluation	The consumer's appraisal of the product or brand on important attributes is called evaluation.
Tangibles	Dimension of service quality-appearance of physical facilities, equipment, personnel, and communication materials are called tangibles.
Tangible	Having a physical existence is referred to as the tangible. Personal property other than real estate, such as cars, boats, stocks, or other assets.

Go to **Cram101.com** for the Practice Tests for this Chapter.
And, **NEVER** highlight a book again!

Personal selling	Personal selling is interpersonal communication, often face to face, between a sales representative and an individual or group, usually with the objective of making a sale.
Forming	The first stage of team development, where the team is formed and the objectives for the team are set is referred to as forming.
Advertisement	Advertisement is the promotion of goods, services, companies and ideas, usually by an identified sponsor. Marketers see advertising as part of an overall promotional strategy.
Production	The creation of finished goods and services using the factors of production: land, labor, capital, entrepreneurship, and knowledge.
Insurance	A means for persons and businesses to protect themselves against the risk of loss is insurance.
Assessment	Collecting information and providing feedback to employees about their behavior, communication style, or skills is an assessment.
Economy	The income, expenditures, and resources that affect the cost of running a business and household are called an economy.
Exchange	The trade of things of value between buyer and seller so that each is better off after the trade is called the exchange.
Voice of the customer	A term that refers to the wants, opinions, perceptions, and desires of the customer is a voice of the customer.
Small business	Small business refers to a business that is independently owned and operated, is not dominant in its field of operation, and meets certain standards of size in terms of employees or annual receipts.

Go to **Cram101.com** for the Practice Tests for this Chapter.
And, **NEVER** highlight a book again!

Information system	An information system is a system whether automated or manual, that comprises people, machines, and/or methods organized to collect, process, transmit, and disseminate data that represent user information.
Servqual	A survey instrument designed to assess service quality along five specific dimensions consisting of tangibles, reliability, responsiveness, assurance, and empathy is referred to as servqual.
Productivity	Productivity refers to the total output of goods and services in a given period of time divided by work hours.
Gross domestic product	The total value of goods and services produced in a country in a given year is a gross domestic product. It is one of several measures of the size of its economy.
Product	Any physical good, service, or idea that satisfies a want or need is called product. Product in project management is a physical entity created as a result of project work.
Mistake	In contract law a mistake is incorrect understanding by one or more parties to a contract and may be used as grounds to invalidate the agreement. Common law has identified three different types of mistake in contract: unilateral mistake, mutual mistake, and common mistake.
Consumer price index	Monthly statistics that measure changes in the prices of about 400 goods and services that consumers buy are called a consumer price index.
Price index	A price index is any single number calculated from an array of prices and quantities over a period. Since not all prices and quantities of purchases can be recorded, a representative sample is used instead.
Consumer	A consumer is a individual or household that consume goods and services generated within the economy. Since this includes just about everyone, the term is a political term as much as an economic term when it is used in everyday speech.
Efficiency	Efficiency refers to the use of minimal resources, such as raw materials, money, and people- to produce a desired volume of output.
Stock	In financial terminology, stock is the capital raized by a corporation, through the issuance and sale of shares. A shareholder is any person or organization which owns one or more shares of a corporation's stock. The aggregate value of a corporation's issued shares is its market capitalization.
Competition	In business, competition occurs when rival organizations with similar products and services attempt to gain customers.
Evaluation	The consumer's appraisal of the product or brand on important attributes is called evaluation.
Purchasing	Purchasing refers to the function in a firm that searches for quality material resources, finds the best suppliers, and negotiates the best price for goods and services.
Market share	The ratio of sales revenue of the firm to the total sales revenue of all firms in the industry, including the firm itself is the market share.
Yield	The interest rate that equates a future value or an annuity to a given present value is a yield.
Marketing	The American Marketing Association suggests that Marketing is "the process of planning and executing the pricing, promotion, and distribution of goods, ideas, and services to create exchanges that satisfy individual and organizational goals."
Users	Users refer to people in the organization who actually use the product or service purchased by the buying center.

Go to **Cram101.com** for the Practice Tests for this Chapter.
And, **NEVER** highlight a book again!

Trust	Trust refers to a legal relationship in which a person who has legal title to property has the duty to hold it for the use or benefit of another person. The term is also used in a general sense to mean confidence reposed in one person by another.
Insurance	A means for persons and businesses to protect themselves against the risk of loss is insurance.
Consumer market	All the individuals or households that want goods and services for personal consumption or use are a consumer market.
Quality control	The measurement of products and services against set standards is referred to as quality control.
Production	The creation of finished goods and services using the factors of production: land, labor, capital, entrepreneurship, and knowledge.
Management	Management characterizes the process of leading and directing all or part of an organization, often a business, through the deployment and manipulation of resources. Early twentieth-century management writer Mary Parker Follett defined management as "the art of getting things done through people."
Mass media	Mass media refers to non-personal channels of communication that allow a message to be sent to many individuals at one time.
Advertising	Advertising refers to paid, nonpersonal communication through various media by organizations and individuals who are in some way identified in the advertising message.
Manager	A person who is formally responsible for supporting the work efforts of other people is a manager.
Interest	Interest refers to the payment the issuer of the bond makes to the bondholders for use of the borrowed money. It is the return to capital achieved over time or as the result of an event.
Closing	The finalization of a real estate sales transaction that passes title to the property from the seller to the buyer is referred to as a closing. Closing is a sales term which refers to the process of making a sale. It refers to reaching the final step, which may be an exchange of money or acquiring a signature.
Communication	Communication refers to the social process in which two or more parties exchange information and share meaning.
Upward communication	A communication channel that allows for relatively free movement of messages from those lower in the organization to those at higher levels is an upward communication.
Personnel	A collective term for all of the employees of an organization. Personnel is also commonly used to refer to the personnel management function or the organizational unit responsible for administering personnel programs.
Hierarchy	A system of grouping people in an organization according to rank from the top down in which all subordinate managers must report to one person is called a hierarchy.
Complexity	The technical sophistication of the product and hence the amount of understanding required to use it is referred to as complexity. It is the opposite of simplicity.
Contact personnel	The people at the 'front lines' who interact with the public in a service setting are contact personnel.
Customer service	The ability of logistics management to satisfy users in terms of time, dependability, communication, and convenience is called the customer service.
Trial	An examination before a competent tribunal, according to the law of the land, of the facts or law put in issue in a cause, for the purpose of determining such issue is a trial. When the

Go to **Cram101.com** for the Practice Tests for this Chapter.
And, **NEVER** highlight a book again!

court hears and determines any issue of fact or law for the purpose of determining the rights of the parties, it may be considered a trial.

Revenue	Revenue refers to the total amount of money a business earns in a given period by selling goods and services. The value of what is received for goods sold, services rendered.
Categorizing	The act of placing strengths and weaknesses into categories in generic internal assessment is called categorizing.
Market segments	Market segments refer to the groups that result from the process of market segmentation; these groups ideally have common needs and will respond similarly to a marketing action.
Automation	Automation allows machines to do work previously accomplished by people.
Malcolm Baldrige National Quality Award	Malcolm Baldrige national quality award refers to U.S. national quality award sponsored by the U.S. Department of Commerce and private industry. The program aims to reward quality in the business sector, health care, and education, and was inspired by the ideas of Total Quality Management.
Electronic commerce	Electronic commerce or e-commerce, refers to any activity that uses some form of electronic communication in the inventory, exchange, advertisement, distribution, and payment of goods and services.
Commerce	Commerce is the exchange of something of value between two entities. It is the central mechanism from which capitalism is derived.
Content	Content refers to all digital information included on a website, including the presentation form-text, video, audio, and graphics.
Customer contact	Customer contact refers to a characteristic of services that notes that customers tend to be more involved in the production of services than they are in manufactured goods.
Participation	Participation refers to the process of giving employees a voice in making decisions about their own work.
Exchange	The trade of things of value between buyer and seller so that each is better off after the trade is called the exchange.
Corporation	A form of business organization that is owned by owners, called shareholders, who have no inherent right to manage the business, and is managed by a board of directors that is elected by the shareholders is called a corporation.
Loyalty	Marketers tend to define customer loyalty as making repeat purchases. Some argue that it should be defined attitudinally as a strongly positive feeling about the brand.
Horizontal communication	The lateral or diagonal exchange of messages among peers or coworkers is referred to as horizontal communication.
Quality dimension	A quality dimension refers to aspects of quality that help to better define what quality is. These include perceived quality, conformance, reliability, durability, and so on.
Focus group	A small group of people who meet under the direction of a discussion leader to communicate their opinions about an organization, its products, or other given issues is a focus group.
Tangibles	Dimension of service quality-appearance of physical facilities, equipment, personnel, and communication materials are called tangibles.
Tangible	Having a physical existence is referred to as the tangible. Personal property other than real estate, such as cars, boats, stocks, or other assets.
Empathy	Empathy refers to dimension of service quality-caring individualized attention provided to customers.

Go to **Cram101.com** for the Practice Tests for this Chapter.

Go to **Cram101.com** for the Practice Tests for this Chapter.
And, **NEVER** highlight a book again!

Industry	Industry refers to a group of firms offering products that are close substitutes for each other.
Forming	The first stage of team development, where the team is formed and the objectives for the team are set is referred to as forming.
Level of service	The degree of service provided to the customer by self, limited, and full-service retailers is referred to as the level of service.
Assessment	Collecting information and providing feedback to employees about their behavior, communication style, or skills is an assessment.
Property	Property refers to something that is capable of being owned. A right or interest associated with something that gives the owner the ability to exercise dominion over it.
Financial risk	The risk related to the inability of the firm to meet its debt obligations as they come due is called financial risk.
Respondent	Respondent refers to a term often used to describe the party charged in an administrative proceeding. The party adverse to the appellant in a case appealed to a higher court.
Objection	In the trial of a case the formal remonstrance made by counsel to something that has been said or done, in order to obtain the court's ruling thereon is an objection.
Jury	A body of lay persons, selected by lot, or by some other fair and impartial means, to ascertain, under the guidance of the judge, the truth in questions of fact arising either in civil litigation or a criminal process is referred to as jury.
Argument	The discussion by counsel for the respective parties of their contentions on the law and the facts of the case being tried in order to aid the jury in arriving at a correct and just conclusion is called argument.
E-business	E-business refers to work an organization does using electronic linkages; any business that takes place by digital processes over a computer network rather than in a physical space.
Layout	Layout refers to the physical arrangement of the various parts of an advertisement including the headline, subheads, illustrations, body copy, and any identifying marks.
Options	Options give the owner the right but not the obligation to buy or sell an underlying security at a set price for a given time period.
Personalization	The consumer-initiated practice of generating content on a marketer's website that is custom tailored to an individual's specific needs and preferences is called personalization.
Competitor	Other organizations in the same industry or type of business that provide a good or service to the same set of customers is referred to as a competitor.
Complaint	The pleading in a civil case in which the plaintiff states his claim and requests relief is called complaint. In the common law, it is a formal legal document that sets out the basic facts and legal reasons that the filing party (the plaintiffs) believes are sufficient to support a claim against another person, persons, entity or entities (the defendants) that entitles the plaintiff(s) to a remedy (either money damages or injunctive relief).
Voice of the customer	A term that refers to the wants, opinions, perceptions, and desires of the customer is a voice of the customer.
Cognitive dissonance	The anxiety a person experiences when he or she simultaneously possesses two sets of knowledge or perceptions that are contradictory or incongruent is referred to as the cognitive dissonance.
Quality measures	Ratios that are used to measure a firm's performance in the area of quality management are referred to as quality measures.

Go to **Cram101.com** for the Practice Tests for this Chapter.

Go to **Cram101.com** for the Practice Tests for this Chapter.
And, **NEVER** highlight a book again!

Comprehensive	A comprehensive refers to a layout accurate in size, color, scheme, and other necessary details to show how a final ad will look. For presentation only, never for reproduction.
Conformance	A dimension of quality that refers to the extent to which a product lies within an allowable range of deviation from its specification is called the conformance.
Teamwork	That which occurs when group members work together in ways that utilize their skills well to accomplish a purpose is called teamwork.
Team building	A term that describes the process of identifying roles for team members and helping the team members succeed in their roles is called team building.
Enabling	Enabling refers to giving workers the education and tools they need to assume their new decision-making powers.
Per capita	A distribution of property in which each member of a group shares equally is per capita.
Continuous improvement	Constantly improving the way the organization does things so that customer needs can be better satisfied is referred to as continuous improvement.
Extension	Extension refers to an out-of-court settlement in which creditors agree to allow the firm more time to meet its financial obligations. A new repayment schedule will be developed, subject to the acceptance of creditors.
Retailing	All activities involved in selling, renting, and providing goods and services to ultimate consumers for personal, family, or household use is referred to as retailing.
Levy	At common law, a levy on goods consisted of an officer's entering the premises where they were and either leaving an assistant in charge of them or removing them after taking an inventory. Today, courts differ as to what is a valid levy, but by the weight of authority there must be an actual or constructive seizure of the goods. In most states, a levy on land must be made by some unequivocal act of the officer indicating the intention of singling out certain real estate for the satisfaction of the debt.

Go to **Cram101.com** for the Practice Tests for this Chapter.
And, **NEVER** highlight a book again!

Best efforts	Best efforts refer to a distribution in which the investment banker agrees to work for a commission rather than actually underwriting the issue for resale. It is a procedure that is used by smaller investment bankers with relatively unknown companies. The investment banker is not directly taking the risk for distribution.
Tangibles	Dimension of service quality-appearance of physical facilities, equipment, personnel, and communication materials are called tangibles.
Tangible	Having a physical existence is referred to as the tangible. Personal property other than real estate, such as cars, boats, stocks, or other assets.
Intangibility	A unique element of services-services cannot be held, touched, or seen before the purchase decision which is referred to as intangibility.
Evaluation	The consumer's appraisal of the product or brand on important attributes is called evaluation.
Inseparability	Inseparability is a characteristic of services, which describes how service products tend to be produced at the same time as they are consumed.
Preparation	Preparation refers to usually the first stage in the creative process. It includes education and formal training.
Customer service	The ability of logistics management to satisfy users in terms of time, dependability, communication, and convenience is called the customer service.
Outbound	Communications originating inside an organization and destined for customers, prospects, or other people outside the organization are called outbound.
Agent	One who acts under the direction of a principal for the principal's benefit in a legal relationship known as agency is called agent.
Brand	A name, symbol, or design that identifies the goods or services of one seller or group of sellers and distinguishes them from the goods and services of competitors is a brand.
Compensation	A payment that is given or recieved as reparation for a service or loss is referred to as compensation.
Closing	The finalization of a real estate sales transaction that passes title to the property from the seller to the buyer is referred to as a closing. Closing is a sales term which refers to the process of making a sale. It refers to reaching the final step, which may be an exchange of money or acquiring a signature.
Case study	A case study is a particular method of qualitative research. Rather than using large samples and following a rigid protocol to examine a limited number of variables, case study methods involve an in-depth, longitudinal examination of a single instance or event: a case. They provide a systematic way of looking at events, collecting data, analyzing information, and reporting the results.
Draft	A signed, written order by which one party instructs another party to pay a specified sum to a third party, at sight or at a specific date is a draft.
Personnel	A collective term for all of the employees of an organization. Personnel is also commonly used to refer to the personnel management function or the organizational unit responsible for administering personnel programs.
Management	Management characterizes the process of leading and directing all or part of an organization, often a business, through the deployment and manipulation of resources. Early twentieth-century management writer Mary Parker Follett defined management as "the art of getting things done through people."

Go to **Cram101.com** for the Practice Tests for this Chapter.

Go to **Cram101.com** for the Practice Tests for this Chapter.
And, **NEVER** highlight a book again!

Bankruptcy	The state of a person who is unable to pay his or her debts without respect to time is called bankruptcy.
Retailing	All activities involved in selling, renting, and providing goods and services to ultimate consumers for personal, family, or household use is referred to as retailing.
Stock	In financial terminology, stock is the capital raized by a corporation, through the issuance and sale of shares. A shareholder is any person or organization which owns one or more shares of a corporation's stock. The aggregate value of a corporation's issued shares is its market capitalization.
Marketing	The American Marketing Association suggests that Marketing is "the process of planning and executing the pricing, promotion, and distribution of goods, ideas, and services to create exchanges that satisfy individual and organizational goals."
Preference	The act of a debtor in paying or securing one or more of his creditors in a manner more favorable to them than to other creditors or to the exclusion of such other creditors is a preference. In the absence of statute, a preference is perfectly good, but to be legal it must be bona fide, and not a mere subterfuge of the debtor to secure a future benefit to himself or to prevent the application of his property to his debts.
Mistake	In contract law a mistake is incorrect understanding by one or more parties to a contract and may be used as grounds to invalidate the agreement. Common law has identified three different types of mistake in contract: unilateral mistake, mutual mistake, and common mistake.
Exhibit	Exhibit refers to a copy of a written instrument on which a pleading is founded, annexed to the pleading and by reference made a part of it. Any paper or thing offered in evidence and marked for identification.
Social responsibility	Social responsibility is a doctrine that claims that an entity whether it is state, government, corporation, organization or individual has a responsibility to society.
Complaint	The pleading in a civil case in which the plaintiff states his claim and requests relief is called complaint. In the common law, it is a formal legal document that sets out the basic facts and legal reasons that the filing party (the plaintiffs) believes are sufficient to support a claim against another person, persons, entity or entities (the defendants) that entitles the plaintiff(s) to a remedy (either money damages or injunctive relief).
Product	Any physical good, service, or idea that satisfies a want or need is called product. Product in project management is a physical entity created as a result of project work.
Communication	Communication refers to the social process in which two or more parties exchange information and share meaning.
Competition	In business, competition occurs when rival organizations with similar products and services attempt to gain customers.
Word of mouth	People influencing each other during their face-to-face converzations is called word of mouth.
Purchasing	Purchasing refers to the function in a firm that searches for quality material resources, finds the best suppliers, and negotiates the best price for goods and services.
Damages	The sum of money recoverable by a plaintiff who has received a judgment in a civil case is called damages.
Discount	A discount is the reduction of the base price of a product.
Bottom line	Bottom line refers to the last line in a profit and loss statement; it refers to net profit.
Contact	The people at the 'front lines' who interact with the public in a service setting are contact

Go to **Cram101.com** for the Practice Tests for this Chapter.

101

Go to **Cram101.com** for the Practice Tests for this Chapter.
And, **NEVER** highlight a book again!

personnel	personnel.
Content	Content refers to all digital information included on a website, including the presentation form-text, video, audio, and graphics.
Customer contact	Customer contact refers to a characteristic of services that notes that customers tend to be more involved in the production of services than they are in manufactured goods.
Corporation	A form of business organization that is owned by owners, called shareholders, who have no inherent right to manage the business, and is managed by a board of directors that is elected by the shareholders is called a corporation.
Corporate culture	The whole collection of beliefs, values, and behaviors of a firm that send messages to those within and outside the company about how business is done is the corporate culture.
Trust	Trust refers to a legal relationship in which a person who has legal title to property has the duty to hold it for the use or benefit of another person. The term is also used in a general sense to mean confidence reposed in one person by another.
Empowerment	Giving employees the authority and responsibility to respond quickly to customer requests is called empowerment.
Regulation	Regulation refers to restrictions state and federal laws place on business with regard to the conduct of its activities.
Forming	The first stage of team development, where the team is formed and the objectives for the team are set is referred to as forming.
Distributive justice	Distributive justice concerns what is just or right with respect to the allocation of goods (or utility) in a society.
Interactional justice	A concept of justice referring to the interpersonal nature of how the outcomes were implemented is referred to as interactional justice.
Coupon	In finance, a coupon is "attached" to bonds, either physically (as with old bonds) or electronically. Each coupon represents a predetermined payment promized to the bond-holder in return for his or her loan of money to the bond-issuer. The bond-holder is typically not the original lender, but receives this payment for effectively lending the money. The coupon rate (the amount promized per dollar of the face value of the bond) helps determine the interest rate or yield on the bond.
Ancillary	An ancillary receiver is a receiver who has been appointed in aid of, and in subordination to, the primary receiver.
Procedural justice	The extent to which the dynamics of an organization's decision-making processes are judged to be fair by those most affected by them is called the procedural justice.
Empathy	Empathy refers to dimension of service quality-caring individualized attention provided to customers.
Consideration	Consideration in contract law, a basic requirement for an enforceable agreement under traditional contract principles, defined in this text as legal value, bargained for and given in exchange for an act or promise. In corporation law, cash or property contributed to a corporation in exchange for shares, or a promise to contribute such cash or property.
Industry	Industry refers to a group of firms offering products that are close substitutes for each other.
Manager	A person who is formally responsible for supporting the work efforts of other people is a manager.
Bond	A long-term debt security that is secured by collateral is called a bond.

Go to **Cram101.com** for the Practice Tests for this Chapter.

Go to **Cram101.com** for the Practice Tests for this Chapter.
And, **NEVER** highlight a book again!

Publicity	Publicity refers to any information about an individual, product, or organization that's distributed to the public through the media and that's not paid for or controlled by the seller.
Categorizing	The act of placing strengths and weaknesses into categories in generic internal assessment is called categorizing.
Hierarchy	A system of grouping people in an organization according to rank from the top down in which all subordinate managers must report to one person is called a hierarchy.
Customer retention	Customer retention refers to the percentage of customers who return to a service provider or continue to purchase a manufactured product.
Patronage	The power of elected and appointed officials to make partisan appointments to office or to confer contracts, honors, or other benefits on their political supporters. Patronage has always been one of the major tools by which political executives consolidate their power and attempt to control a bureaucracy.
Demographics	Demographics is a shorthand term for 'population characteristics'. Demographics include race, age, income, mobility (in terms of travel time to work or number of vehicles available), educational attainment, home ownership, employment status, and even location. Demographics are primarily used in economic and marketing research.
Demographic	A demographic is a term used in marketing and broadcasting, to describe a demographic grouping or a market segment.
Intervention	A proceeding by which one not originally made a party to an action or suit is permitted, on his own application, to appear therein and join one of the original parties in maintaining his cause of action or defense, or to assert some cause of action against some or all of the parties to the proceeding as originally instituted is an intervention.
Competitor	Other organizations in the same industry or type of business that provide a good or service to the same set of customers is referred to as a competitor.
Tactic	A short-term immediate decision that, in its totality, leads to the achievement of strategic goals is called a tactic.
Contingency approach	Contingency approach refers to the dominant perspective in organizational behavior, it argues that there's no single best way to manage behavior. What 'works' in any given context depends on the complex interplay between a variety of person and situational factors.

Go to **Cram101.com** for the Practice Tests for this Chapter.
And, **NEVER** highlight a book again!

Customer retention	Customer retention refers to the percentage of customers who return to a service provider or continue to purchase a manufactured product.
Management	Management characterizes the process of leading and directing all or part of an organization, often a business, through the deployment and manipulation of resources. Early twentieth-century management writer Mary Parker Follett defined management as "the art of getting things done through people."
Tactic	A short-term immediate decision that, in its totality, leads to the achievement of strategic goals is called a tactic.
Manager	A person who is formally responsible for supporting the work efforts of other people is a manager.
Financial ratio	A financial ratio is a ratio of two numbers of reported levels or flows of a company. It may be two financial flows categories divided by each other (profit margin, profit/revenue). It may be a level divided by a financial flow (price/earnings). It may be a flow divided by a level (return on equity or earnings/equity). The numerator or denominator may itself be a ratio (PEG ratio).
Inventory	Inventory refers to physical material purchased from suppliers, which may or may not be reworked for sale to customers. A unique element of services-the need for and cost of having a service provider available.
Evaluation	The consumer's appraisal of the product or brand on important attributes is called evaluation.
Marketing	The American Marketing Association suggests that Marketing is "the process of planning and executing the pricing, promotion, and distribution of goods, ideas, and services to create exchanges that satisfy individual and organizational goals."
Targeting	Targeting refers to the ability to address personalized promotions to a particular person who may be identified or described by means of an anonymous profile.
Product	Any physical good, service, or idea that satisfies a want or need is called product. Product in project management is a physical entity created as a result of project work.
Competition	In business, competition occurs when rival organizations with similar products and services attempt to gain customers.
Value-added services	Services provided by an intermediary that make the original product more valuable and may generate additional revenue for the intermediary are referred to as value-added services.
Value-added	A customer-based perspective on quality that is used by services, manufacturing, and public sector organizations is value-added. The concept of value-added involves a subjective assessment of the efficacy of every step in the process for the customer.
Partnership	In the common law, a partnership is a type of business structure in which partners share with each other the profits or losses of the business undertaking in which they have all invested.
Insurance	A means for persons and businesses to protect themselves against the risk of loss is insurance.
Brand	A name, symbol, or design that identifies the goods or services of one seller or group of sellers and distinguishes them from the goods and services of competitors is a brand.
Policy	Similar to a script in that a policy can be a less than completely rational decision-making method. Involves the use of a pre-existing set of decision steps for any problem that presents itself.
Brand loyalty	The degree to which customers are satisfied, like the brand, and are committed to further

Go to **Cram101.com** for the Practice Tests for this Chapter.

Go to **Cram101.com** for the Practice Tests for this Chapter.
And, **NEVER** highlight a book again!

	purchase is referred to as brand loyalty.
Loyalty	Marketers tend to define customer loyalty as making repeat purchases. Some argue that it should be defined attitudinally as a strongly positive feeling about the brand.
Marketing strategy	Marketing strategy refers to the means by which a marketing goal is to be achieved, usually characterized by a specified target market and a marketing program to reach it.
Promotion	Promotion refers to all the techniques sellers use to motivate people to buy products or services. An attempt by marketers to inform people about products and to persuade them to participate in an exchange.
Sales promotion	Sales promotion refers to the promotional tool that stimulates consumer purchasing and dealer interest by means of short-term activities.
Inseparability	Inseparability is a characteristic of services, which describes how service products tend to be produced at the same time as they are consumed.
Level of service	The degree of service provided to the customer by self, limited, and full-service retailers is referred to as the level of service.
Discount	A discount is the reduction of the base price of a product.
Client	The organizations with the products, services, or causes to be marketed and for which advertising agencies and other marketing promotional firms provide services is referred to as a client.
Industry	Industry refers to a group of firms offering products that are close substitutes for each other.
Honor	Payment of a drawer's properly drawn check by the drawee bank is referred to as honor.
Advertising	Advertising refers to paid, nonpersonal communication through various media by organizations and individuals who are in some way identified in the advertising message.
Bottom line	Bottom line refers to the last line in a profit and loss statement; it refers to net profit.
Mass marketing	Mass marketing refers to developing products and promotions to please large groups of people.
Abandonment	Abandonment in law, the relinquishment of an interest, claim, privilege or possession. This broad meaning has a number of applications in different branches of law.
Users	Users refer to people in the organization who actually use the product or service purchased by the buying center.
Financial market	In economics, a financial market is a mechanism which allows people to trade money for securities or commodities such as gold or other precious metals. In general, any commodity market might be considered to be a financial market, if the usual purpose of traders is not the immediate consumption of the commodity, but rather as a means of delaying or accelerating consumption over time.
Stock	In financial terminology, stock is the capital raized by a corporation, through the issuance and sale of shares. A shareholder is any person or organization which owns one or more shares of a corporation's stock. The aggregate value of a corporation's issued shares is its market capitalization.
Customer service	The ability of logistics management to satisfy users in terms of time, dependability, communication, and convenience is called the customer service.
Acquisition	A company's purchase of the property and obligations of another company is an acquisition.
Expense	An expense refers to costs involved in operating a business, such as rent, utilities, and salaries.

Go to **Cram101.com** for the Practice Tests for this Chapter.

Go to **Cram101.com** for the Practice Tests for this Chapter.
And, **NEVER** highlight a book again!

Target audience	That group that composes the present and potential prospects for a product or service is called the target audience.
Direct marketing	Promotional element that uses direct communication with consumers to generate a response in the form of an order, a request for further information, or a visit to a retail outlet is direct marketing.
Target market	One or more specific groups of potential consumers toward which an organization directs its marketing program are a target market.
Marketing intermediaries	Independent firms that assist in moving goods and services from producers to industrial and consumer users are marketing intermediaries.
Channel	Channel, in communications (sometimes called communications channel), refers to the medium used to convey information from a sender (or transmitter) to a receiver.
Distribution	Distribution is one of the four aspects of marketing. A distribution business is the middleman between the manufacturer and retailer or (usually)in commercial or industrial the business customer.
Retailing	All activities involved in selling, renting, and providing goods and services to ultimate consumers for personal, family, or household use is referred to as retailing.
Channel of distribution	A whole set of marketing intermediaries, such as wholesalers and retailers, who join together to transport and store goods in their path from producers to consumers is referred to as channel of distribution.
Agent	One who acts under the direction of a principal for the principal's benefit in a legal relationship known as agency is called agent.
Premium	Premium refers to the fee charged by an insurance company for an insurance policy. The rate of losses must be relatively predictable: In order to set the premium (prices) insurers must be able to estimate them accurately.
Purchasing	Purchasing refers to the function in a firm that searches for quality material resources, finds the best suppliers, and negotiates the best price for goods and services.
Market share	The ratio of sales revenue of the firm to the total sales revenue of all firms in the industry, including the firm itself is the market share.
Competitive advantage	A business is said to have a competitive advantage when its unique strengths, often based on cost, quality, time, and innovation, offer consumers a greater percieved value and there by diffetiating it from its competitors.
Interest	Interest refers to the payment the issuer of the bond makes to the bondholders for use of the borrowed money. It is the return to capital achieved over time or as the result of an event.
Broker	An agent who bargains or carries on negotiations in behalf of the principal as an intermediary between the latter and third persons in transacting business relative to the acquisition of contractual rights, or to the sale or purchase of property the custody of which is not entrusted to him or her for the purpose of discharging the agency is called a broker.
Holder	A person in possession of a document of title or an instrument payable or indorsed to him, his order, or to bearer is a holder.
Debit	Debit is a formal bookkeeping and accounting term that comes from the Latin word debere, which means "to owe".
Cooperative	A business owned and controlled by the people who use it, producers, consumers, or workers with similar needs who pool their resources for mutual gain is called cooperative.

Go to **Cram101.com** for the Practice Tests for this Chapter.
And, **NEVER** highlight a book again!

Extension	Extension refers to an out-of-court settlement in which creditors agree to allow the firm more time to meet its financial obligations. A new repayment schedule will be developed, subject to the acceptance of creditors.
Price war	Successive price-cutting by competitors to increase or maintain their unit sales or market share is a price war.
Intangibility	A unique element of services-services cannot be held, touched, or seen before the purchase decision which is referred to as intangibility.
Management philosophy	Management philosophy refers to a philosophy that links key goal-related issues with key collaboration issues to come up with general ways by which the firm will manage its affairs.
Competitor	Other organizations in the same industry or type of business that provide a good or service to the same set of customers is referred to as a competitor.
Customer contact	Customer contact refers to a characteristic of services that notes that customers tend to be more involved in the production of services than they are in manufactured goods.
Trust	Trust refers to a legal relationship in which a person who has legal title to property has the duty to hold it for the use or benefit of another person. The term is also used in a general sense to mean confidence reposed in one person by another.
Content	Content refers to all digital information included on a website, including the presentation form-text, video, audio, and graphics.
Efficiency	Efficiency refers to the use of minimal resources, such as raw materials, money, and people-to produce a desired volume of output.
Production	The creation of finished goods and services using the factors of production: land, labor, capital, entrepreneurship, and knowledge.
Property	Property refers to something that is capable of being owned. A right or interest associated with something that gives the owner the ability to exercise dominion over it.
Contract	A contract is a "promise" or an "agreement" that is enforced or recognized by the law. In the civil law, contracts are considered to be part of the general law of obligations. This article describes the law relating to contracts in common law jurisdictions.
Communication	Communication refers to the social process in which two or more parties exchange information and share meaning.
Relationship marketing	Marketing whose goal is to keep individual customers over time by offering them products that exactly meet their requirements is called relationship marketing.
Mortgage	A conveyance of property to secure the performance of some obligation, the conveyance to be void on the due performance thereof is referred to as the mortgage.
Patronage	The power of elected and appointed officials to make partisan appointments to office or to confer contracts, honors, or other benefits on their political supporters. Patronage has always been one of the major tools by which political executives consolidate their power and attempt to control a bureaucracy.
Bond	A long-term debt security that is secured by collateral is called a bond.
Business risk	The risk related to the inability of the firm to hold its competitive position and maintain stability and growth in earnings is business risk.
Customer database	Customer database refers to a computer database specifically designed for storage, retrieval, and analysis of customer data by marketers.
Continuous	Constantly improving the way the organization does things so that customer needs can be

Go to **Cram101.com** for the Practice Tests for this Chapter.

Go to **Cram101.com** for the Practice Tests for this Chapter.
And, **NEVER** highlight a book again!

improvement	better satisfied is referred to as continuous improvement.
Personnel	A collective term for all of the employees of an organization. Personnel is also commonly used to refer to the personnel management function or the organizational unit responsible for administering personnel programs.
Bar code	Bar code refers to a printed code that makes use of lines of various widths to encode data about products.
Empathy	Empathy refers to dimension of service quality-caring individualized attention provided to customers.
Tangibles	Dimension of service quality-appearance of physical facilities, equipment, personnel, and communication materials are called tangibles.
Tangible	Having a physical existence is referred to as the tangible. Personal property other than real estate, such as cars, boats, stocks, or other assets.
Word of mouth	People influencing each other during their face-to-face converzations is called word of mouth.
Perceived risk	The anxieties felt because the consumer cannot anticipate the outcomes of a purchase but believes that there may be negative consequences is called a perceived risk.
Refunding	The process of retiring an old bond issue before maturity and replacing it with a new issue is refunding. Refunding will occur when interest rates have fallen and new bonds may be sold at lower interest rates.
Contact personnel	The people at the 'front lines' who interact with the public in a service setting are contact personnel.
Consideration	Consideration in contract law, a basic requirement for an enforceable agreement under traditional contract principles, defined in this text as legal value, bargained for and given in exchange for an act or promise. In corporation law, cash or property contributed to a corporation in exchange for shares, or a promise to contribute such cash or property.
Buyer	A buyer refers to a role in the buying center with formal authority and responsibility to select the supplier and negotiate the terms of the contract.
Acceptance	The actual or implied receipt and retention of that which is tendered or offered is the acceptance.
Total Quality Management	The practice of striving for customer satisfaction by ensuring quality from all departments in an organization is called total quality management.
Quality management	Quality management is a method for ensuring that all the activities necessary to design, develop and implement a product or service are effective and efficient with respect to the system and its performance.
Net present value	Net present value refers to the present value of the cash inflows minus the present value of the cash outflows with the cost of capital used as a discount rate. This method is used to evaluate capital budgeting projects.
Present value	Present value refers to the current or discounted value of a future sum or annuity. The value is discounted back at a given interest rate for a specified time period.
Customer value	Customer value refers to the unique combination of benefits received by targeted buyers that includes quality, price, convenience, on-time delivery, and both before-sale and after-sale service.
Customer defection	Customer defection refers to customers who do not continue to purchase from the enterprise. The words attrition and churn are often used to describe the same phenomenon.

Go to **Cram101.com** for the Practice Tests for this Chapter.

Go to **Cram101.com** for the Practice Tests for this Chapter.
And, **NEVER** highlight a book again!

Monopoly	A market in which there is only one seller is referred to as monopoly.
Brand equity	The combination of factors such as awareness, loyalty, perceived quality, images, and emotions people associate with a given brand name is referred to as brand equity.
Equity	Equity is the name given to the set of legal principles, in countries following the English common law tradition, which supplement strict rules of law where their application would operate harshly, so as to achieve what is sometimes referred to as "natural justice."
Incentive	A reward offered by a marketer to a prospective customer in return for furnishing information or making a purchase is referred to as an incentive.
Closing	The finalization of a real estate sales transaction that passes title to the property from the seller to the buyer is referred to as a closing. Closing is a sales term which refers to the process of making a sale. It refers to reaching the final step, which may be an exchange of money or acquiring a signature.
Voice of the customer	A term that refers to the wants, opinions, perceptions, and desires of the customer is a voice of the customer.
Small business	Small business refers to a business that is independently owned and operated, is not dominant in its field of operation, and meets certain standards of size in terms of employees or annual receipts.
Marketing management	Marketing management refers to the process of planning and executing the conception, pricing, promotion, and distribution of ideas, goods, and services to create mutually beneficial exchanges.
Yield	The interest rate that equates a future value or an annuity to a given present value is a yield.
Annual report	Annual report refers to a yearly statement of the financial condition and progress of an organization.
Departmental-zation	The dividing of organizational functions into separate units is called departmentalization.
Organizational culture	Widely shared values within an organization that provide coherence and cooperation to achieve common goals are referred to as a organizational culture.
Audit	Audit refers to the verification of a company's books and records pursuant to federal securities laws, state laws, and stock exchange rules that must be performed by an independent CPA.
Contribution	In business organization law, the cash or property contributed to a business by its owners is referred to as contribution.

Go to **Cram101.com** for the Practice Tests for this Chapter.

Go to **Cram101.com** for the Practice Tests for this Chapter.
And, **NEVER** highlight a book again!

Departmental-zation	The dividing of organizational functions into separate units is called departmentalization.
Marketing	The American Marketing Association suggests that Marketing is "the process of planning and executing the pricing, promotion, and distribution of goods, ideas, and services to create exchanges that satisfy individual and organizational goals."
Advertising campaign	A comprehensive advertising plan that consists of a series of messages in a variety of media that center on a single theme or idea is referred to as an advertising campaign.
Advertising	Advertising refers to paid, nonpersonal communication through various media by organizations and individuals who are in some way identified in the advertising message.
Recruitment	Recruitment refers to the set of activities used to obtain a sufficient number of the right people at the right time; its purpose is to select those who best meet the needs of the organization.
Personnel	A collective term for all of the employees of an organization. Personnel is also commonly used to refer to the personnel management function or the organizational unit responsible for administering personnel programs.
Competitor	Other organizations in the same industry or type of business that provide a good or service to the same set of customers is referred to as a competitor.
Contact personnel	The people at the 'front lines' who interact with the public in a service setting are contact personnel.
Inseparability	Inseparability is a characteristic of services, which describes how service products tend to be produced at the same time as they are consumed.
Human resources	Human resources refers to the individuals within the firm, and to the portion of the firm's organization that deals with hiring, firing, training, and other personnel issues.
Planning horizon	The length of time it takes to conceive, develop, and complete a project and to recover the cost of the project on a discounted cash flow basis is referred to as planning horizon.
Innovation	The process of creating and doing new things that are introduced into the marketplace as products, processes, or services is innovation.
Production	The creation of finished goods and services using the factors of production: land, labor, capital, entrepreneurship, and knowledge.
Customer service	The ability of logistics management to satisfy users in terms of time, dependability, communication, and convenience is called the customer service.
Insurance	A means for persons and businesses to protect themselves against the risk of loss is insurance.
Agent	One who acts under the direction of a principal for the principal's benefit in a legal relationship known as agency is called agent.
Property	Property refers to something that is capable of being owned. A right or interest associated with something that gives the owner the ability to exercise dominion over it.
Marketing orientation	When an organization focuses its efforts on continuously collecting information about customers' needs and competitors' capabilities, sharing this information across departments, and using the information to create customer value, we have marketing orientation.
Product	Any physical good, service, or idea that satisfies a want or need is called product. Product in project management is a physical entity created as a result of project work.
Promotion	Promotion refers to all the techniques sellers use to motivate people to buy products or

Go to **Cram101.com** for the Practice Tests for this Chapter.

Go to **Cram101.com** for the Practice Tests for this Chapter.
And, **NEVER** highlight a book again!

	services. An attempt by marketers to inform people about products and to persuade them to participate in an exchange.
Efficiency	Efficiency refers to the use of minimal resources, such as raw materials, money, and people- to produce a desired volume of output.
Agency	Agency refers to a legal relationship in which an agent acts under the direction of a principal for the principal's benefit. Also used to refer to government regulatory bodies of all kinds.
Premium	Premium refers to the fee charged by an insurance company for an insurance policy. The rate of losses must be relatively predictable: In order to set the premium (prices) insurers must be able to estimate them accurately.
Customer contact	Customer contact refers to a characteristic of services that notes that customers tend to be more involved in the production of services than they are in manufactured goods.
Client	The organizations with the products, services, or causes to be marketed and for which advertising agencies and other marketing promotional firms provide services is referred to as a client.
Economies of scale	A decline in costs with accumulated sales or production is an economies of scale. In advertising, economies of scale often occur in media purchases as the relative costs of advertising time and/or space may decline as the size of the media budget increases.
Centralization	A structural policy in which decision-making authority is concentrated at the top of the organizational hierarchy is referred to as centralization.
Operations management	A specialized area in management that converts or transforms resources into goods and services is operations management.
Management	Management characterizes the process of leading and directing all or part of an organization, often a business, through the deployment and manipulation of resources. Early twentieth-century management writer Mary Parker Follett defined management as "the art of getting things done through people."
Coordination	Coordination refers to the set of mechanisms used in an organization to link the actions of its subunits into a consistent pattern.
Competencies	An organization's special capabilities, including skills, technologies, and resources that distinguish it from other organizations are competencies.
Authority	Authority in agency law, refers to an agent's ability to affect his principal's legal relations with third parties. Also used to refer to an actor's legal power or ability to do something. In addition, sometimes used to refer to a statute, case, or other legal source that justifies a particular result.
Competitive Strategy	An outline of how a business intends to compete with other firms in the same industry is called competitive strategy.
Contribution	In business organization law, the cash or property contributed to a business by its owners is referred to as contribution.
Competitive advantage	A business is said to have a competitive advantage when its unique strengths, often based on cost, quality, time, and innovation, offer consumers a greater percieved value and there by differtiating it from its competitors.
Holder	A person in possession of a document of title or an instrument payable or indorsed to him, his order, or to bearer is a holder.
Discount	A discount is the reduction of the base price of a product.

Go to **Cram101.com** for the Practice Tests for this Chapter.
And, **NEVER** highlight a book again!

Communication	Communication refers to the social process in which two or more parties exchange information and share meaning.
Target market	One or more specific groups of potential consumers toward which an organization directs its marketing program are a target market.
Mass production	The process of making a large number of a limited variety of products at very low cost is referred to as mass production.
Competition	In business, competition occurs when rival organizations with similar products and services attempt to gain customers.
Options	Options give the owner the right but not the obligation to buy or sell an underlying security at a set price for a given time period.
Status quo	The existing state of things is the status quo. In contract law, returning a party to status quo or status quo ante means putting him in the position he was in before entering the contract.
Participation	Participation refers to the process of giving employees a voice in making decisions about their own work.
Channel	Channel, in communications (sometimes called communications channel), refers to the medium used to convey information from a sender (or transmitter) to a receiver.
Trust	Trust refers to a legal relationship in which a person who has legal title to property has the duty to hold it for the use or benefit of another person. The term is also used in a general sense to mean confidence reposed in one person by another.
Leverage	Leverage is using given resources in such a way that the potential positive or negative outcome is magnified. In finance, this generally refers to borrowing.
Brand	A name, symbol, or design that identifies the goods or services of one seller or group of sellers and distinguishes them from the goods and services of competitors is a brand.
Corporation	A form of business organization that is owned by owners, called shareholders, who have no inherent right to manage the business, and is managed by a board of directors that is elected by the shareholders is called a corporation.
Interpersonal skills	Interpersonal skills are used to communicate with, understand, and motivate individuals and groups.
Market segments	Market segments refer to the groups that result from the process of market segmentation; these groups ideally have common needs and will respond similarly to a marketing action.
Layout	Layout refers to the physical arrangement of the various parts of an advertisement including the headline, subheads, illustrations, body copy, and any identifying marks.
Quality control	The measurement of products and services against set standards is referred to as quality control.
Comparative advantage	The ability one country to produce a good at a lower cost, relative to other goods, compared to other countries. A counrty is said to have a comparative advantage over another country in the production of one good as opposed to another if its relative efficiency in the production of that good is higher than the other country's.
Evaluation	The consumer's appraisal of the product or brand on important attributes is called evaluation.
Manager	A person who is formally responsible for supporting the work efforts of other people is a manager.

Go to **Cram101.com** for the Practice Tests for this Chapter.

Go to **Cram101.com** for the Practice Tests for this Chapter.
And, **NEVER** highlight a book again!

Compensation	A payment that is given or recieved as reparation for a service or loss is referred to as compensation.
Organizational culture	Widely shared values within an organization that provide coherence and cooperation to achieve common goals are referred to as a organizational culture.
Change agent	A change agent is someone who engages either deliberately or whose behavior results in social, cultural or behavioral change. This can be studied scientifically and effective techniques can be discovered and employed.
Restructuring	Restructuring is the corporate management term for the act of partially dismantling and reorganizing a company for the purpose of making it more efficient and therefore more profitable.
General manager	A manager who is responsible for several departments that perform different functions is called general manager.
Revenue	Revenue refers to the total amount of money a business earns in a given period by selling goods and services. The value of what is received for goods sold, services rendered.
Empowerment	Giving employees the authority and responsibility to respond quickly to customer requests is called empowerment.
Context	The effect of the background under which a message often takes on more and richer meaning is a context. Context is especially important in cross-cultural interactions because some cultures are said to be high context or low context.
Facilitator	A facilitator is someone who skilfully helps a group of people understand their common objectives and plan to achieve them without personally taking any side of the argument.
Audit	Audit refers to the verification of a company's books and records pursuant to federal securities laws, state laws, and stock exchange rules that must be performed by an independent CPA.
Loyalty	Marketers tend to define customer loyalty as making repeat purchases. Some argue that it should be defined attitudinally as a strongly positive feeling about the brand.
Certificates of deposit	Certificates of deposit refer to a certificate offered by banks, savings and loans, and other financial institutions for the deposit of funds at a given interest rate over a specified time period.
Bond	A long-term debt security that is secured by collateral is called a bond.
Customer retention	Customer retention refers to the percentage of customers who return to a service provider or continue to purchase a manufactured product.
Users	Users refer to people in the organization who actually use the product or service purchased by the buying center.
Servqual	A survey instrument designed to assess service quality along five specific dimensions consisting of tangibles, reliability, responsiveness, assurance, and empathy is referred to as servqual.
Productivity	Productivity refers to the total output of goods and services in a given period of time divided by work hours.
Downsizing	The process of eliminating managerial and non-managerial positions are called downsizing.
Continuity	A media scheduling strategy where a continuous pattern of advertising is used over the time span of the advertising campaign is continuity.
External	Dealers, who buy products to sell to others, and ultimate customers, who buy products for

Go to **Cram101.com** for the Practice Tests for this Chapter.
And, **NEVER** highlight a book again!

customers	their own personal use are referred to as external customers.
Franchise	A business established or operated under an authorization to sell or distribute a company's goods or services in a particular area is a franchise.
Information technology	Information technology refers to technology that helps companies change business by allowing them to use new methods.
Corporate culture	The whole collection of beliefs, values, and behaviors of a firm that send messages to those within and outside the company about how business is done is the corporate culture.
Organization culture	The set of values that helps the organization's employees understand which actions are considered acceptable and which unacceptable is referred to as the organization culture.
Bottom line	Bottom line refers to the last line in a profit and loss statement; it refers to net profit.
Closing	The finalization of a real estate sales transaction that passes title to the property from the seller to the buyer is referred to as a closing. Closing is a sales term which refers to the process of making a sale. It refers to reaching the final step, which may be an exchange of money or acquiring a signature.
Marketing strategy	Marketing strategy refers to the means by which a marketing goal is to be achieved, usually characterized by a specified target market and a marketing program to reach it.
Industry	Industry refers to a group of firms offering products that are close substitutes for each other.

Go to **Cram101.com** for the Practice Tests for this Chapter.

Go to **Cram101.com** for the Practice Tests for this Chapter.
And, **NEVER** highlight a book again!

Printed in the United Kingdom
by Lightning Source UK Ltd.
117588UKS00001B/36